CO-AZX-255

BRITAIN

THE QUEEN ♔ CRICKET 🏏
🎩🔍 SHERLOCK HOLMES
AND OTHER THINGS ☕🗡
INDUBITABLY
BRITISH

BRITAIN

THE QUEEN CRICKET SHERLOCK HOLMES AND OTHER THINGS INDUBITABLY BRITISH

Norman Kolpas, Consulting Editor

A Running Press / Friedman Group Book

Running Press
Philadelphia, Pennsylvania

A RUNNING PRESS / FRIEDMAN GROUP BOOK

Copyright © 1987 by Michael Friedman Publishing Group, Inc.

All rights reserved. No part of this publication may be reproduced, stored in a retrieval system, or transmitted, in any form or by any means, electronic, mechanical, photocopying, recording, or otherwise, without the prior written permission of the copyright owner.

International representatives:
Worldwide Media Services, Inc.
115 East 23rd Street
New York, NY 10010

9 8 7 6 5 4 3 2 1

Digit on the right indicates the number of this printing.

Library of Congress Cataloging in Publication Number
87-60184

ISBN 0-89471-534-8 Cloth

The following publishers have generously given permission to use material from copyrighted works: The poem on page 65, "A Ballad of the Investiture 1969" from *Collected Poems*, appears with permission by John Murray Publishers, © 1974 by John Betjeman. Illustration by Ernest H. Shepard on page 72 from *The Wind In The Willows* by Kenneth Grahame. Illustrations copyright 1933 Charles Scribner's Sons; copyright renewed © 1961 Ernest H. Shepard. Reprinted with the permission of Charles Scribner's Sons.

Britain
The Queen, Cricket, Sherlock Holmes, and Other Things Indubitably British
was prepared and produced by
Michael Friedman Publishing Group, Inc.
15 West 26th Street
New York, New York 10010

Consulting Editor: Norman Kolpas
Editor: Pamela Hoenig/Louise Quayle
Art Director: Mary Moriarty
Designer: Robert W. Kosturko
Photo Researcher: Susan Trangmar
Photo Editor: Philip Hawthorne
Production Manager: Karen L. Greenberg

Typeset by BPE Graphics, Inc.
Color separations by Hong Kong Scanner Craft Company Ltd.
Printed and bound in Hong Kong by Leefung Asco Printers Ltd.

This book may be ordered from the publisher.
Please include $1.50 postage.
But try your bookstore first!

Running Press
125 South 22nd Street
Philadelphia, PA 19103

Author Credits

John Brookes
Public Parks and Gardens; Great Private Gardens; A Nation of Gardeners

Mike Brown
Ancient Stones; The Chelsea Flower Show; Televised Masterpieces; Televised Mayhem; Seaside Resorts

Debbie Geller
"Four Lads That Shook the World;" Visual Music

Tim Heald
Unconventional Sleuths; Fleet Street; The Derby and Royal Ascot; Polo and the Hunt; Thames River Sports; Life Itself: Cricket; Rougher Sports: Soccer and Rugby; The Bus and Underground

Tara Heinemann
Cottages: Life on a Human Scale

Philip Inwood
Stately Homes; Rural and Romantic Traditions; Contemporary Artists

Sylvia Katz
Castles and Cathedrals

Norman Kolpas
Food and Drink; Poets Laureate; Other Tongues, Other Literatures; Charles Dickens; Children's Literature: A Little Girl, a Bunny, a Toad, and a Bear; *Theater;* The Sport of the Linksland; The Lawn Tennis Championships; Automobiles of Luxury: Rolls-Royce; Automobiles of Sport; Country Rambles; "Half the Fun"

Robin May
Folk Traditions; Great Performers and Performances; A Cinematic Legacy

Carol Timperley
The Cutting Edge of Fashion; The Princess Di Look

Geoffrey Warren
Royal and Democratic Heroes; A Piece of Royalty; Interior Design: "The Quest for Comfort"; Pottery and Porcelain; Furniture: Its Golden Age to the Modern Traditionalists; Country Crafts; Wearing the Colors of the Clan; The Country Look

Christopher Warwick
A Modern Monarchy; Pomp and Pageantry

About the Authors

JOHN BROOKES is one of Britain's leading landscape designers, a noted educator, and an author. He holds a Diploma in Landscape Design from University College, London, and has been in private practice since 1964. He has completed landscape work for both public and private clients in the United Kingdom, the Channel Islands, the Continent and the United States. His many books include *Room Outside, Gardens for Small Spaces, The Small Garden*, and *A Place in the Country*. John Brookes lives in Fontwell, near Arundel, West Sussex.

MIKE BROWN was born and raised in Cape Town, South Africa. In 1970, he emigrated to Britain, where he became a naturalized citizen. He served as a staff writer in the London office of Time-Life Books for six years, working on such series as "The World's Wild Places," "The Great Cities" and "The British Empire." He continues to freelance as a writer and editor for a number of British publishers. Mike Brown is also an accomplished artist, whose etchings have been exhibited in London at the Royal Academy of Arts Summer Exhibition and at the Camden Institute. He lives and works in London.

DEBBIE GELLER is a New Yorker and a former staffer with *Rolling Stone* magazine. She currently lives in London, where she works as a writer/producer specializing in popular music (among other topics) for the British Broadcasting Corporation's arts program, "Arena."

TIM HEALD was born in Dorchester, Dorset, and was educated at Sherborne and at Balliol College, Oxford. His distinguished career in British journalism has included positions as Feature Writer for the *Daily Express* in London and Foreign Correspondent (North America) for the *Daily Telegraph*. He is currently a freelance writer for leading British newspapers and magazines. He has written more than sixteen nonfiction and fiction books, including *The Character of Cricket, Networks—Who We Know and How We Use Them*, and the Simon Bognor series of crime novels, serialized in Britain by Thames TV. He also contributes short stories to various anthologies and to the *Ellery Queen Mystery Magazine*. Tim Heald lives in Richmond, near London.

TARA HEINEMANN worked in the photographic archives of the National Portrait Gallery, London, before becoming a professional freelance photographer in 1977. Since then, she has specialized in photographing writers for leading British and American publishers, newspapers, and magazines. Her portraits are widely exhibited, and she has recently finished a book of photographs and interviews with Britons from all walks of life who were born in 1900. Tara Heinemann lives with her husband, the painter Philip Inwood, in a seventeenth-century thatched cottage in North Oxfordshire.

PHILIP INWOOD was born in Hong Kong and studied Fine Art at the Bath Academy of Art. He currently serves as Lecturer in the History of Art at Wroxton College, Oxfordshire—an overseas campus of Fairleigh Dickinson University (New Jersey). He was included in the 1981 Young Contemporaries show at the Institute of Contemporary Art in London, and his paintings are now regulary exhibited throughout Britain. Inwood lives with his wife, the photographer Tara Heinemann, in North Oxfordshire.

SYLVIA KATZ received her degree in the History of Art and Architecture from Bristol University. She trained in furniture design at the Hornsey College of Art in London, and has worked as a furniture and graphic designer. She writes on design and materials for a wide variety of publications, and is a leading expert on plastic design items—of which she has a vast collection and about which she has written three books. Sylvia Katz lives with her husband and two sons in London, where she currently works for the Design Council.

NORMAN KOLPAS was born in Chicago and raised in Los Angeles. He studied English Literature at Yale University and, upon graduation, he moved to London where he lived for seven years. In England, he worked as a staff writer and editor for Time-Life Books and was a freelance writer for such publications as *The Times*, *Time Out*, and the *International Herald-Tribune*. He returned to the U.S. in 1980, where he served first as Managing Editor of Cuisinart's *The Pleasures of Cooking* magazine and then as Editor of The Knapp Press in Los Angeles. He is the author of seven nonfiction books including, *The Coffee Lover's Companion*, *The Chocolate Lover's Companion*, *The Gourmet's Lexicon*, and biographies of Abraham Lincoln and Chairman Mao. Norman Kolpas now lives in Los Angeles and is married to the novelist Katie Goldman.

ROBIN MAY is a British author and journalist who specializes in writing about the performing arts and the American West. His interest in the latter grew out of his early addiction to American history: he was among the first British schoolchildren to study it during World War II. He has written some fifty books for adults and young people (opera and the Indian Wars are his particular passions), and his long-term project is a biography of the Mohawk Indian, Joseph Brant. He is married, has three children, and currently lives in Wimbledon.

CAROL TIMPERLEY was educated at Durham University, where she studied English Language and Literature. She went on to Manchester University as a research assistant on a dictionary of English landscape, and in 1984, she was a part of the editorial team that launched the British magazine *Working Woman*. Since 1985, she has been Staff Writer of *A la carte* magazine. Carol Timperley lives in London.

GEOFFREY WARREN studied art in Portsmouth and London, obtaining the National Diploma in Design. He served as Art Editor of British *Vogue* and other women's magazines, and his experience with antiques led to his appointment as Antiques Editor of *Candida* magazine. Geoffrey Warren now works full-time as a freelance writer and contributes articles to a number of leading British magazines. His books include *Royal Souvenirs*, *Victorian and Edwardian Needlecraft*, *Vanishing Street Furniture*, *Kitchen Bygones*, and *An Encyclopedia of Fashion Accessories* (which includes his own illustrations). He lives in London.

CHRISTOPHER WARWICK was born in London in 1949. He is acknowledged to be an authority on British royalty, and appears frequently on British television and radio. He began a full-time writing career in 1980, and has since published seven books on modern royal history, including such best-selling titles as *Princess Margaret* (written in collaboration with Her Royal Highness), *King George VI & Queen Elizabeth* (voted one of the best books of 1985), *Debrett's Queen Elizabeth II* and *Abdication* (a reappraisal of the lives of the Duke and Duchess of Windsor). Christopher Warwick lives in Wimbledon, near London.

Contents

Introduction

Rule Britannia
Britannia rules the waves!
Britons never, never, never
Shall be slaves!

Thus begin the lyrics to "Rule Britannia!," easily the most popular British patriotic song after "God Save the Queen." To this day, Britons sing the anthem with praise, inspiration, and, not too surprisingly, with conviction, as well, whether they're attending a Royal Wedding, a British football victory at Wembley Stadium, or taking part in a friendly get-together at the local pub. The song recalls an age when England was a dominant power in the world, an age when her people were subjects to no one. And, listening to the song sung today, one suddenly realizes that the singers *still believe the lyrics to be true.* Though the Empire is long past, though the nation's economic greatness has declined, Britain is *still* one of the most influential countries on earth. It holds strong sway over our cultural tastes, our lifestyles, and our leisure time. Its history and its current affairs continue to capture the world's imagination.

This book is a celebration of the many ways in which Britain continues to influence the world. In an impressionistic, visual, and textural account, *Britain* sets out to define what it is about Britain and the British people that sets them apart, that makes them seem not just different but somehow "better" in many ways. While the chapters of the book are broken down into broad subject categories—gardens, architecture and interiors, music, literature, food and drink, and so on—there are strong aspects of what we'll call "Britishness" that transcend specific topics. Page by page, specific topics are highlighted within each broad subject area that define Britain. In effect, the following offers not one, but over fifty different approaches to defining what it is about Britain that is quintessentially British.

Heritage and tradition, for example, are characteristics integral to a British sensibility. Britons, even the most forward-looking ones, are guided by a very strong sense of what has come before. Tradition manifests itself in so many ways—in the comfort of modern British interior design; in the wood panelling and the dartboard of a country pub; in the monoliths of Stonehenge; and in the world-class theater company dedicated to the works of William Shakespeare, with its headquarters in the city of his birth.

Patriotism, too, is closely related to tradition. The red, white, and blue bars of the Union Jack fly proudly throughout the nation, and drape the heads and shoulders of spectators at international football matches. Bold public monuments and statues celebrate Britain's heroes. The Queen and the Royal Family are celebrated and revered.

They stand both as symbols of what is best and most noble about the country and its people, and at the same time, constitute the most lavish, complex, and entertaining live soap opera ever staged for the public's enjoyment. The audience, needless to say, is international.

A sense of and a striving for excellence is another all-pervasive British characteristic. Beer, cheeses, tweeds, tartans, automobiles, pottery—you cannot speak of British products without, in the same breath, speaking of their unchallenged quality. Tradition and patriotism are closely tied to success in these areas: British workmen, craftsmen, and artists, in upholding their national pride, have a strong sense of doing things as they have always been done in the past. British actors speak more of their "craft" than of their "art," regarding stagecraft as something to be done with the highest standards in mind. A sports commentator will describe a cricket or tennis match with low-key words like "nice" and "well-played," bringing an air of fine assessment to the game. Listeners or viewers can't help but begin to "see," with a new appreciation, the skill, the finely honed talent, the quality in action.

And then there's eccentricity. The British are known as much for their incredible dottiness—and their matter-of-fact acceptance of it—as for anything else. Reruns of the "Monty Python" show attest to this fact, especially when one considers their Ministry of Silly Walks routine involving a bunch of bowler-hatted British government men who walk with the gaits of inebriated cranes. Many British detectives of fiction, particularly Sherlock Holmes, are the great eccentrics of world literature. Think of the imagination it took for A. A. Milne to create Winnie-the-Pooh, or for Kenneth Grahame to create Toad and Mole and Ratty. Consider four young musicians from Liverpool who would change the way the world thought of popular music, while incidentally making mop-top haircuts the tonsorial statement of the early 1960s. Britons are known for lovingly tending elaborate gardens on the tiniest patches of land. The ideal holiday is often a seven-day tramp across the wilds of the Lake District, and who but a Briton would get all misty-eyed at the televising of the Last Night of the annual summer Promenade Concerts ("The Proms") at the Royal Albert Hall? Individualists? Yes! Eccentrics? Most definitely!

Tradition. Patriotism. Quality. Eccentricity. You'll find these characteristics tossed together in varying proportions in a distinctly British fashion. These are the ingredients that charm us when we consider Britain and its people. And with good reason—they're what make Britain a land that is one of the proudest and most revered in the world.

—Norman Kolpas

Chapter 1

Heritage and Royalty

Ancient Stones

MODERN BRITONS, BY AND LARGE, take pride in the antiquity of their island culture. The most famous embodiment of their ancient past, and the object of their deepest pride, rises from the bleak expanse of Salisbury Plain in the county of Wiltshire in southern England. The Bronze Age monument of Stonehenge, built by a pre-Celtic people between 3100 and 1100 B.C., is the grandest of Britain's roughly nine hundred stone circles. In spite of the volumes written about it, no one yet knows for sure what purpose Stonehenge really served— observatory, temple, tribal center, or perhaps all three —for the generations who have flocked to it.

What is certain is that Stonehenge remains one of Britain's top prehistoric attractions, drawing in excess of 600,000 tourists a year. The unfortunate upshot of such fame is that visitors can no longer wander freely among the megaliths (stone slabs weighing as much as forty-five tons) for fear that the stones might be stroked, scuffed, or graffiti-etched down to the size of pebbles. Even so, Stonehenge retains a brooding power that is best experienced when few folks are around, preferably in the off-season on a stormy winter's day.

Substantial, though uncounted, numbers of Britons strongly believe in the mystical and esoteric signifi-

cance of the nation's ancient sites. Until recently, white-robed members of the modern Ancient Order of Druids celebrated the annual summer solstice at Stonehenge, in the belief that sun-worship ceremonies were held there four thousand years ago.

Stonehenge aside, Britain's widely varied ancient legacy includes some two thousand megalithic tombs, three thousand Iron Age hill forts, and a galaxy of burial mounds, or barrows, and single standing stones "hoary and lichened by age, grim and fretted by a thousand storms" (as the turn-of-the-century writer Walter Johnson melodramatically put it in his 1908 book *Folk-Memory*). Scat-

tered across the length and breadth of the country, most are reasonably accessible to twentieth-century visitors, though a car is often essential for tracking them down. To come across an ancient monument is a strangely moving experience, whether on a bleak moor, in a village churchyard, or, like the remnants of London's Roman Wall, in the orbit of modern urban office buildings.

Some of the richest concentrations of sites are to be found in southern England. Perhaps the most important cluster centers on the five-thousand-year-old Avebury stone circles in Wiltshire, not far from Stonehenge; they cover a twenty-eight-acre

English Heritage

The Castlerigg Stone Circle, near Keswick, in Cumbria, has stood among the stormy peaks of England's Lake District for some fifty centuries. Considerably smaller than Stonehenge, only eight of its forty-eight stones (thirty-eight in the outer circle, ten in an inner rectangle) exceed five feet (1.5 meters) in height.

BTA

English Heritage

Britain's most renowned ancient sites seem to have become a part of the nation's natural landscape. Snaking across the bleak moors of Northumberland, Hadrian's Wall (above), begun in 122 A.D. under the reign of the Emperor Hadrian, is the most impressive monument remaining of Rome's rule over Britain. The stone circle known as Stonehenge (right), on the Salisbury Plain in southern England, is the greatest of all ancient monuments; its original purpose has inspired speculation since the beginning of history.

area and enclose a part of tiny Avebury village. In the same region are found the 330-foot-long West Kennett Long Barrow, a multi-chambered tomb built around 3250 B.C., and Silbury Hill, Europe's largest prehistoric artificial mound. At Maiden Castle in Dorset, energetic walkers may roam Britain's greatest Neolithic hill fort, whose forty-nine acres are encompassed by mighty defensive earthworks. Of Roman remains, the most dramatic is Hadrian's Wall, which snakes for seventy-three miles

over the hills of Northumberland; constructed between 122 and 125 A.D., it marked the northern frontier of Roman Britain.

Two of the most unusual and widely contrasting sites can be found at opposite ends of the country. At Cerne Abbas in Dorset, a 180-foot-high outline of a naked club-wielding giant, dating from about the second century A.D., has been cut into the chalk hillside; its prominent sexual organ, some thirty feet in length, reputedly made it a magnet for fertility

rites. And at Skara Brae on the remote Orkney Islands off the coast of Scotland, adventurous travelers can explore the interiors of Bronze Age homes, complete with megalithic beds, dressers, and hearths.

Whatever the nature of the ancient sites, so much about them remains unknown and unknowable that they will continue to grip the imaginations of both Britons and foreign visitors. Like the enigmatic British themselves, the stones defy complete analysis or understanding.

Royal and Democratic Heroes

IT'S NO WONDER THAT A COUNTRY ruled for centuries by God-chosen monarchs should have hero-worship so deeply engrained in its national character. Although they stand in awe of majesty, the British, ever contrary, also want their monarchs to possess the "human" touch, and a monarch who manages to appear at once exalted and down-to-earth can achieve stratospheric heights of popularity.

Elizabeth I was one of the first British monarchs to gain such distinction. Although an autocratic ruler, she knew when to bend and be gracious. Her name is now inseparable from the years of her reign in British history; the "Elizabethan Age" was thought then, and is still considered, a "golden" age.

Queen Victoria also gave her name to an age, though it was not until the later years of her reign that she became truly popular—old age being a virtue the British respect in their leaders. There was great rejoicing at Victoria's Golden Jubilee in 1887; when, aged seventy-eight, she celebrated her Diamond Jubilee in 1897, the public's adoration was boundless. Reminders of her huge popularity remain legion, from the Victoria Monument outside Buckingham Palace to innumerable statues all over not only Britain but also what was once the Empire. Thoroughfares,

National Portrait Gallery, London

parks, hotels, and even a London railway station bear her name to this day in honor of her reign.

The Scots still hark to the memory of "Bonnie Prince Charlie." Prince Charles Edward Stuart made an abortive bid for the British throne in 1745, only to see it dashed at the Battle of Culloden. Scottish hearts still show their tenderness for his valiant deeds in popular lyrics such as the "Skye Boating Song" and "Will Ye No' Come Back Again?"

The British prefer the man of action to the artist or the thinker. A touch of bravado, a mysterious or scandalous private life, and, best of all, a brave or violent death guarantee enshrinement in the public heart. Being an island people, the British rank sailors high—and none higher, both literally and figuratively, than Admiral Lord Nelson atop his column in Trafalgar Square in London. A brilliant commander and defier of authority (who turned his "blind eye" at the Battle of Copenhagen), he made Lady Hamilton his mistress and died a glorious death on board his ship, *Victory,* at the Battle of Trafalgar in 1805. What more could the public want? To this day, Nelson's ship, moored in Portsmouth harbor, is a major attraction.

In British eyes, the archetypal soldier-king is Henry V, who led the country to victory at the Battle of Agincourt in 1415 and whose stirring leadership in the capture of Harfleur was immortalized by Shakespeare in a speech that begins:

> *Once more unto the breach, dear*
> *friends, once more;*
> *Or close the wall up with our*
> *English dead!*

and ends:

> *. . . The game's afoot:*
> *Follow your spirit; and, upon this*
> *charge*
> *Cry "God for Harry! England and*
> *Saint George!"*

Queen Elizabeth I posed regally (left) in a contemporary portrait attributed to John Bettes. Two more recent heroes of less royal, but no less noble blood, were Lord Nelson, portrayed in the statue that tops a 170-foot (52-meter) granite column in Trafalgar Square (right), and Sir Winston Churchill (below), whose bulldog determination saw Britain through World War II's most trying times.

BTA

National Portrait Gallery, London

A more modern British military hero is the Duke of Wellington, who defeated Napoleon at the Battle of Waterloo in 1815. His London home, Apseley House, now the Wellington Museum, is a treasure trove of memorabilia. A London railway station and bridge commemorate his famous victory, and the present £5 note carries his portrait.

A military hero of a different sort, but nonetheless British, was T.E. Lawrence, or, as he is better known, Lawrence of Arabia. The self-styled leader of the Arab Revolt against the Ottoman Empire during World War I, Lawrence was a fearless soldier, a brilliant writer, and a man who seemed both to aggressively seek and determinedly shun and despise fame. He remains one of history's most romantic and enigmatic figures.

As the birthplace of the "Mother of Parliaments," Britain has bred many heroic upholders of the democratic ideal. Not surprisingly, wartime prime ministers—William Pitt during the Napoleonic era or David Lloyd George, the "Welsh Wizard," during World War I—have received the greatest popular acclaim and left Britons with the most stirring memories.

Sir Winston Churchill's stand against Hitler remains, in British memory, the most heroic of all. With his majestic oratory ("We shall fight them on the beaches . . ."), his defiantly jutting cigar, and his "V for Victory" gesture, he seemed at times to be the very embodiment of the spirit of dogged British determination. In many ways, and in many hearts, Churchill remains the quintessential British leader.

A Modern Monarchy

WHEN ASKED TO DEFINE THE AL-lure of the British monarchy, most people find a succinct response diffi-cult, if not impossible. But all are agreed that it holds a mystique as tantalizingly remote, as intangible, as the stars. Monarchy, nevertheless, is an anachronism. In today's world,

how could it possibly be otherwise? Yet, for all that, it is an anachronism perfectly suited to the British way of life, not least because the history of the Crown is the history of its people. And so it has been that the Crown has charted Britain's course for al-most a thousand years.

In fact, it might even be argued that it is only in the collective imagi-nation that the monarchy exists at all, representing a sophisticated form of "adult magic," a brilliant illusion that, like some breathtaking piece of con-juring, delights, entertains, even be-wilders. Essentially, it persuades the common individual that there still remains, in a dangerously cynical world, something out of the ordinary in which to believe.

Of course, the undiminished magic of the monarchy depends, for the most part, on all those who rep-resent it—in short, those members of the royal family whose names and faces are as familiar to the British as those of their own friends and rela-tions, and whose lives, which speak of another world, never fail to gener-ate phenomenal interest.

Is it this, perhaps, that turns the legs of lesser mortals to jelly, that finds those waiting to meet members of the royal family shivering with nerves or hopelessly tongue-tied, un-able to recall more than a few words addressed to them? Who can say? But one fact, no matter how absurd, remains perfectly clear: the royal "spell" has much the same devastat-ing effect on people from all levels of society, from hardened politicians to the most newsworthy celebrities and public figures, from nonchalant so-cialites who have seen it all to the or-dinary man in the street.

Decorative though the monarchy most certainly is, its many functions are as valid today—perhaps even

Portrait Study by Karsh of Ottawa/Camera Press, London

Members of the Royal Family are the most popular photo-graphic subjects in the nation. Queen Elizabeth II and her husband Philip, Duke of Edin-burgh (left) are frequently snapped in the ornate setting of Buckingham Palace. As soon as the engagement was announced of the Queen's sec-ond son, Prince Andrew, to Miss Sarah Ferguson (right) in 1986, she was religiously stalked by photographers. The young Princes William (next in line to the throne after his father, Prince Charles) and Harry (far right), posed with their parents for a portrait by Lord Snowdon, ex-husband of the queen's sister, Princess Margaret.

Snowdon/Camera Press, London

Camera Press, London

more so—as at any time in its long existence. Yet, while devoted to the interests and well-being of the nation as a whole (royal patronage actively encompasses every stratum of British life, from the finely tuned world of the arts to basic, everyday matters of social welfare), the monarchy's prime function, in all its subtle guises, may be its work in the field of diplomacy. As ambassadors, members of the royal family—and in particular the Queen herself—are frequently more successful in handling delicate issues and in promoting Britain's interests abroad than any diplomat.

To have been able to survive in a turbulent, radically changing world, where acceptable standards are often questioned, if not ridiculed, the institution of the monarchy has had to prove itself capable of adapting to the times. In guiding it along a course that past kings could never have imagined possible, no British sovereign has been more astute or successful than Elizabeth II herself. A disarmingly modest and unassuming woman, Elizabeth has brought the monarchy sharply into the twentieth century. As a result of her efforts, it has transcended all manner of social barriers so that, today, it is within reach of the common man.

In Her Majesty's quest to keep the royal ideal alive, the monarchy is now represented by an increasing number of individuals who, in spite of the royal titles bestowed upon them by the Crown, are not of royal birth. With the disappearance of most of the world's monarchies through war, revolution, or plain disenchantment, royal marriages in the truest sense have

Albert Watson/Camera Press, London

With the Royal Family so much in the public spotlight, it's all too easy to forget that they actually are real people and a close family. Four generations gathered together for the wedding of Prince Andrew and Sarah Ferguson on July 23, 1986 (left). The Queen often strikes a more relaxed pose, as in this picture with one of her favorite dogs, a corgi (right). Most approachable and widely loved of all the royals is undoubtedly the Queen Mother (mother of Queen Elizabeth II and Princess Margaret), who posed with four of her grandchildren (Charles, Edward, Anne, and Andrew) for a warm-hearted portrait on her 85th birthday.

become a thing of the past. Even King George V, that most reactionary of all monarchs, bowed to the inevitable when, as early as 1917, he informed his Privy Council that he would permit his children, the last truly royal "thoroughbreds," to marry members of Britain's aristocratic families, or, as they were once known, "the ruling class." With the exception of only two of his five surviving children—his successor Edward VIII, who as the Duke of Windsor married the American divorcée Wallis Warfield Simpson, and Prince George, Duke

of Kent, who married Princess Marina of Greece and Denmark—the king's offspring did indeed choose partners from Britain's aristocracy. Princess Mary married Henry, Viscount Lascelles, later the Sixth Earl of Harewood; Prince Albert, Duke of York, who upon his brother's abdication in 1936 ascended the throne as King George VI, married Lady Elizabeth Bowes Lyon (now Queen Elizabeth, the Queen Mother), the English-born daughter of the ancient Scottish Strathmore clan; and Prince Henry, Duke of Gloucester, took as

his bride Lady Alice Montagu-Douglas-Scott, daughter of another Scottish family, the Buccleuchs.

Thus the trend toward what might best be described as "semi-royal" alliances continues to the present day, with the acceptability of potential spouses extended from the families of the aristocracy to the landed gentry and the upper-middle classes. The 1960 marriage of the Queen's only sister, Princess Margaret, to society photographer Antony Armstrong-Jones (now the Earl of Snowdon), was followed one year

Norman Parkinson/Camera Press, London

Portrait Study by Karsh of Ottowa/Camera Press, London

later by the wedding of Her Majesty's cousin, Edward, Duke of Kent, to Miss Katharine Worsley, daughter of a Yorkshire squire. In 1963, the Duke of Kent's sister, Princess Alexandra, married the Honourable Angus Ogilvy, a City of London business-man and grandson of Queen Mary's celebrated Lady-in-Waiting, Mabell, Countess of Airlie.

The Queen's children have contin-ued the trend. In November 1973, her daughter, Princess Anne, married Mark Phillips, a captain in the Queen's Dragoon Guards. Eight years later, the search for a suitable bride for the Heir Apparent led to a young kindergarten teacher, Lady Diana Spencer, who assumed the title of Princess of Wales. And the latest royal bride, Miss Sarah Ferguson,

who married the Queen's second son, Prince Andrew, on July 23, 1986, continued to run the London office of a fine art publisher even as preparations for her elevation to royal status were put into motion.

Not so very long ago, kings lived in fear that daylight, if allowed to pen-etrate the musty shadows of so an-cient, even hallowed, an institution as the monarchy, might presage its end in Britain. Queen Elizabeth II has proven such fears groundless. While the nation at large is on a far more intimate footing with its royal family than at any time in the past, it is clear that the gradual introduction of "daylight" has done nothing to dam-age the monarchy's unique form of magic. If anything, the spell it casts has grown even stronger.

A Piece of Royalty

THOUGH THE MODERN ROYAL family has shown the British public a more human face than monarchies of the past, the majority of Britons—not to mention people throughout the world—remain spellbound by its mystique and glamor. People especially crave tangible mementos of important moments in royal lives, and manufacturers throughout Britain have willingly supplied an ever-increasing flood of commemorative objects for public consumption.

For a souvenir of the 1981 wedding of Prince Charles and Lady Diana Spencer, one could have spent as much as £325 on a Wedgwood jasper vase—or as little as 25 pence for a pencil from Woolworth's. Different though they are in form and value, both items exemplify the inherent fascination with all royal collectibles. Emblazoned with portraits or emblems, they offer buyers the extraordinary superimposed upon the ordinary—the exalted and remote made popular and accessible. With such notable exceptions as royal portrait busts, commemorative medals, and miniatures of coronation regalia, virtually all royal collectibles have their commonplace counterparts—from postcards to coffee mugs, teapots to jigsaw puzzles.

Medals were thrown to the crowds lining the route of the coronation procession of Edward VI in 1547, but the earliest-known popular royal souvenir is an English Lambeth Delftware plate, dated 1600. Its inscription—*The rose is red, the leaves are green, God save Elizabeth our Queene*—refers, of course, to Elizabeth I. The later Stuarts and early Hanoverians were crudely portrayed on Delftware platters, and Bonnie Prince Charlie appeared on Jacobite wine glasses in the 1740s; but not until the 1750s, and the invention of cheap transfer-printing on ceramics, was it possible for commemoratives to be manufactured in any number.

Mass-production really got under way with Queen Victoria's coronation in 1837, and mugs from that event are among the rarest of collectibles. As the nineteenth century progressed, so did the Royal Family's popularity—as well as the technical expertise to amply feed the public's growing appetite for royal souvenirs.

This century has seen a profusion of British royal events. There have been four coronations—actually five,

The Design Council

Josiah Wedgwood & Sons Ltd.

Royal souvenirs range from inexpensive everday items to costly collector's pieces. Reigning monarchs and their families have appeared on postcards since Queen Victoria's time (left). The 1981 marriage of Prince Charles to Lady Diana Spencer excited a flood of memorabilia, including such whimsical items as teapots and egg cozies (above). And Wedgwood provided collectors with a framed, limited-edition plaque in white-on-blue Jasperware (right) to commemorate the Queen's 60th birthday in 1986.

if one includes that of Edward VIII, later Duke of Windsor, which never took place (he stepped down from the throne before his 1937 coronation to marry Mrs. Wallace Simpson). Nonetheless, appropriate commemoratives were made in anticipation of the event. Two Silver Jubilees have been celebrated, and there have been so many births, marriages, deaths, special birthdays, and State visits that the souvenir industry has been kept busy and the royalty-hungry world well-supplied.

The ubiquitous mug is the most popular and enduring of all royal collectibles. Most are transfer-printed or painted by unknown artists. But serious collectors look for the mugs designed by the well-known artists Eric Ravilious and Dame Laura Knight for the coronations of Edward VIII and George VI. Beginning with the coronation of Queen Elizabeth II in 1953, every important royal occasion has been commemorated with a Wedgwood mug designed by Professor Guyatt, R.A. (Royal Academy)—including one for the 1986 wedding of Prince Andrew and Miss Sarah Ferguson. Many such special collector's mugs are limited editions, and make worthwhile investments.

Yet the real appeal of royal commemoratives remains the very personal way in which they bring the Royal Family into everyday lives. The Queen, when she was still Princess Elizabeth, was depicted in photographs with her sister, Princess Margaret, on countless ceramics and tumblers; they also appeared together, surprisingly, in relief on a glass jelly mold made in 1937. (Any item featuring the young princesses was very popular.) As the ever-popular Queen Mother continues to age graciously, her birthdays are celebrated by all manner of mugs, vases, and plates. And in 1985, a mug was issued to mark the third and first birthdays, respectively, of Prince William and Prince Henry, the sons of Prince Charles and Princess Diana—proof positive that the tradition of royal collectibles will carry on in future generations.

Pomp and Pageantry

WHILE CERTAIN ASPECTS OF THE British way of life may be equaled, if not bettered, by other nations, Britain's royal pageantry is one feature that stands in a class of its own, unsurpassed anywhere else in the world. If so bold a statement sounds excessively jingoistic, it also happens to be entirely true.

For the most part, British pageants can be said to fall into one of three categories. The most general and common category might include the daily ceremonies of Changing the Guard at Buckingham Palace and Windsor Castle; the simpler Ceremony of the Keys, the nightly changing of the guards at the Tower of London; Beating Retreat, in the Horse Guards Parade in May, with massed military bands and marching; and, to a lesser extent, such annual events as the Lord Mayor's Show, which follows the installation of each Lord Mayor of London on the Saturday nearest November twelfth, and such summertime military displays as the Royal Tournament in London and the Edinburgh Tattoo.

Into the second category fall events of a specifically royal nature. These include the dazzling spectacle of the Sovereign's Birthday Parade, better known as Trooping the Colour (*never* Trooping *of* the Colour, as it is often mistakenly called), on June eleventh or the nearest Saturday; royal weddings; and ceremonies centered around the Orders of Chivalry, notably the Installation of Knights of the Most Noble Order of the Garter, at Windsor.

The last category represents all those events officially designated state occasions. Foremost among them is, of course, the coronation of the sovereign. Then follow the state opening of Parliament in late

October/early November; state visits made by foreign monarchs or heads of state; and, from time to time, state funerals, an honor accorded a king, a queen regnant (reigning queen), or, as happened upon the death of Queen Mary in 1953, a queen consort (wife of a reigning king). Seldom is the honor of a state funeral accorded a non-royal individual, though in 1965 Sir Winston Churchill, former prime minister and elder statesman, was interred at Bladon Churchyard, near Blenheim Palace in Oxfordshire, following a morning of state obsequies solemnly observed at St. Paul's Cathedral in the presence of the entire royal family.

Of all royal ceremonies, coronations are by far the most significant. In a long traditional ritual, based on ancient religious and symbolic rites, the new king or queen regnant is anointed with holy oil, invested with the emblems of sovereignty—the Regalia—and, finally, crowned. By that act is the sovereign considered to have taken full and rightful possession of his or her kingdom, at one with God and the people.

Ancient though the coronation ritual is, the origins of certain other royal ceremonials may also be traced to antiquity. England's premier Order of Chivalry, the Most Noble Order of the Garter, for example, was founded in 1348 by King Edward III, the seventh sovereign of the House of Plantagenet. History relates that while dancing with King Edward, Joan, Countess of Salisbury, contrived to let her blue garter slip from her thigh. Picking it up off the floor, the king turned to his grinning courtiers and admonished them with the words *"Honi soi qui mal y pense"* (Shame on him who thinks evil of it).

As a result of that incident, Edward III established the aptly named Order of the Garter, immediately distinguishable by its broad blue sash or riband traditionally worn over the left shoulder. The "badge" of the Order is an eight-pointed star; at its center, the cross of St. George is encircled by a buckled garter bearing the motto of the Order—that is, the sober words Edward III issued to his followers that April evening more than six hundred years ago. With or without the installation of new knights, a service of Thanksgiving for

British pageantry moves to a complex set of cycles, some daily, some annual, some occurring only infrequently. Once a year in mid-November, the City of London—ancient heart of the lower-case city we now call London—is the scene for the elaborate Lord Mayor's Show, a parade of state coaches and gala floats that celebrates the newly elected Lord Mayor of The City. Its highlight is the passing of the Lord Mayor's Ceremonial Coach (left), resplendently painted and gilded and accompanied by pikemen in traditional dress. Every night at 10 P.M., the yeoman warders at the Tower of London (more commonly called beefeaters), along with army guardsmen, participate in the Ceremony of the Keys (right), locking up the Tower as they have daily since King Henry VII founded the beefeaters in 1485.

Weidenfeld Archive

BTA

Camera Press, London

To celebrate her official birthday on June 13, the Queen, on a Saturday in mid-June each year, receives the salute of a Guards' regiment in the ceremony known as Trooping the Colour (above). While marching bands play, the Queen, in uniform, rides on horseback (left) from Buckingham Palace to the Horseguards' Parade off Whitehall in one of the grandest annual displays of British pageantry.

Beefeaters in traditional Tudor dress (right) lead the procession at St. George's Chapel, Windsor Castle, in the service of Thanksgiving for the Order of the Garter. Each year on the third Monday in June, knights old and new—limited to twenty-four in all—of this premier order of English chivalry pay their homage to the Queen.

Camera Press, London

the Order of the Garter is held at St. George's Chapel, Windsor Castle, every year in June.

Today, an equally traditional ceremony is Trooping the Colour, held in London. Whereas at Windsor, in a setting splendidly evocative of the Middle Ages, the Queen walks in procession in a long robe of deep blue velvet to attend the Garter service, Trooping the Colour requires Her Majesty to wear regimental uniform and ride sidesaddle from Buckingham Palace down the Mall—a distance of 1,821 yards—to Horse Guards Pa-

rade. There, as commander-in-chief, the Queen takes the salute at the world's most exacting, most spectacular military parade, mounted in honor of what has become known as the sovereign's "official birthday."

While the form of the parade we know today dates back to 1755, it did not become so grand, or permanent, a feature of British life until much later. Nor, indeed, was it always purely ceremonial. Once upon a time trooping the "colour"—the regimental standard—through the ranks of foot-soldiers was a matter of vital signifi-

cance. In those long-ago days when cannon, sword, musket, and brute strength were the instruments of warfare, it was essential for each man on the battlefield to familiarize himself with the banner under which he fought. The essential act of trooping the colour, therefore, was one of regimental recognition, and it was common practice right up until 1854, when the Battle of Inkerman was fought in the Crimea.

Today's ceremony is, of course, little more than a symbolic act. The Queen's presence reminds Britons

not only that the armed forces owe direct allegiance to her rather than to the state, but also that in days past the sovereign actually led troops into battle. The last king of England to do so was George II, who rode at the head of his men at the Battle of Dettingen on June 27, 1743.

Such ties to a glorious past are fundamental to the mystique of British pageantry. In a country increasingly subject to international tastes and customs, pageantry is indubitably one aspect of national life that remains quintessentially British.

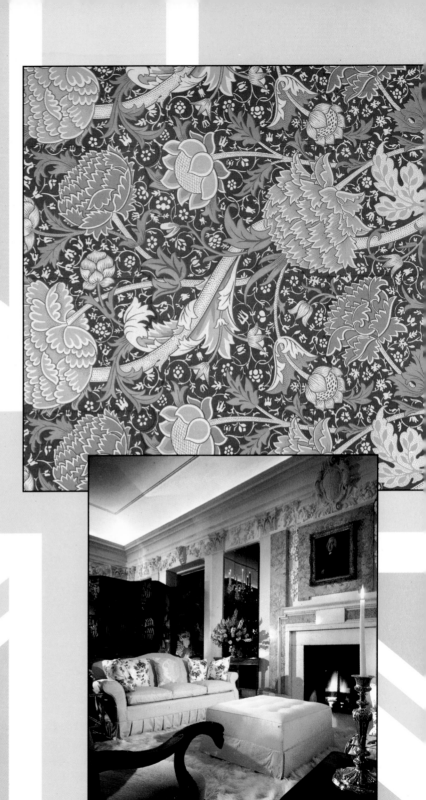

Chapter 2
Architecture and Interior Design

Castles and Cathedrals

English Heritage

The ruined walls of Ashby-de-la-Zouch Castle (left) in Leicestershire evoke a strong, romantic feeling for the past. The castle was built largely during the fourteenth century, and served as a Royalist stronghold during the English Civil War.

Westminster Abbey (below) has been the church of the nation ever since William the Conqueror decided that he would be crowned king there on Christmas Day, 1066. The abbey has changed greatly since then, and is today a Gothic structure dating from the thirteenth and fourteenth centuries.

BTA

THE TWENTIETH CENTURY HAS brought with it anonymous tower blocks and miles of bland motorways, but the architectural heritage of Britain's past echoes with centuries of pomp and ceremony. The construction and interior design of old castles teaches us about the lifestyles of our ancestors, as well as about the ingenuity of their architects and engineers. And what finer way can there be to steep yourself in British history than to visit the country's great castles and cathedrals? Seeing the places where their footsteps passed, textbook characters come alive; the imagination quickens. Was that distant thump a boulder catapulted by a siege machine, or just the sound effects background to a tour commentary?

The true glory of Britain's past is perpetuated in its cathedrals. They offer a fascinating variety of architectural styles, spanning the centuries. Their vaulted ceilings alone are cause for wonder, ranging from solid Norman arcades to decorated Gothic and Perpendicular tracery to soaring fan vaults—some of the most elegant patterns ever created in stone. From the bulk and majesty of Durham Cathedral to the vast elegance of York Minster, from Ely Cathedral shining like a holy beacon on the flat fens of eastern England to the awesome and hallowed Canterbury Cathedral, Britain's holy shrines capture the wonder of its noble past.

Son et lumiere (elaborate light and sound productions) staged for tourists may tend to romanticize the Gothic grandeur of Britain's castles. In reality, they were built to repel violent attacks, and what looks like a stony frill round the top of the castle wall is very likely the pattern work of holes through which fatal doses of burning oil, lead, and sand were poured onto the enemy.

Though such lethal measures are long a thing of the past, many British castles are still private family homes. Most castles, however, are now open to the public, offering something to please every taste: the castellated keep at Eastnor, Hereford, a fake Victorian creation; the fairy tale Scotney Old Castle with its moat in Kent; or Caister Castle, which houses a collection of vintage cars. Then there's Carreg Cennen near Llandeilo, Wales, where torches can be rented to navigate its underground passages. Wandering by flickering light, one can almost imagine a wizard lurking around the next bend, ready to cast his spell; but a spell has already long since been cast by the stones of Britain's glorious history.

Some Outstanding Castles and Cathedrals

Castles

Ashby-de-la-Zouch, Leicestershire. Originally a fortified manor and now a tall, imposing ruin with beautiful fireplaces and exposed windows.

Arundel, West Sussex. Occupied for centuries by the ancestors of the Duke of Norfolk, who still lives there. One of the greatest of all English medieval castles.

Caernarvon, Gwynedd. A fortress castle built with unusual striped brickwork. It embodies the essence of Welsh myth and legend, and was the magnificent setting for the investiture of Charles, Prince of Wales.

Conwy, Gwynedd. This castle has been described as the finest medieval fortress in Britain, if not Europe. Proudly situated at the mouth of the River Conwy, it symbolizes the rugged Welshness of the fortresses built by Edward I. You can walk all the way 'round its ramparts—which are punctuated by eight round towers—and enjoy a panoramic view of the town and river.

Glamis, Angus. Styled like a French chateau, this stunning Scottish castle was the setting for the bloody murder of Shakespeare's Macbeth.

Harlech, Gwynedd. A premier example of the concentric style of castle architecture, perched on a cliff above the Irish Sea. The two great symmetrical entry turrets are in the best sandcastle tradition.

Leeds, Kent. A must for lovers of the picturesque. Set on an island in an artificial lake.

The Tower of London. A fortress that has never been captured. One of the best examples of the grandeur and ostentation of William the Conqueror's architectural schemes. The White Tower is one of the most magnificent stone keeps in Britain.

Windsor, Berkshire. A miniature city, this royal residence is the largest inhabited castle in the world. Its buildings span eight hundred years, presenting an unprecedented visual history of castle design on one site.

Cathedrals

Canterbury, Kent. Steeped in legend, Canterbury is one of the greatest pilgrimage shrines in Europe. Memories of the violent murder of Thomas à Becket at the altar in 1170 contrast strongly with the tranquil cloistered walk, the stained glass, and the finest Norman crypt in Europe.

Durham, Durham. Framed against the sky on a rock above the River Wear, it has been hailed by many as the finest Norman church in England and is filled with fascinating tombs and furnishings.

Ely, Cambridgeshire. Unique in Europe, with its octagonal tower—one of the most amazing engineering feats of the Middle Ages. The lantern soars up from the middle of the cathedral, allowing light to pour down onto the crossing.

Lincoln, Lincolnshire. A breathtaking fourteenth-century cathedral, famed for its immense figured west front, its carved Angel Choir, and the Dean's Eye rose window.

Wells, Somerset. Not merely the cathedral with the greatest number of sculpted figures in Britain on its west front screen, Wells is an almost complete living example of a medieval close—a cathedral encircled by the original houses of the churchmen, which are still occupied. A walk down the cobbled Vicar's Close is a trip back in time. The turreted Bishop's Palace stands guarded by its moat, where swans ring a bell to be fed.

Winchester, Hampshire. The longest cathedral in Europe, resplendent with paintings, glass, fine examples of fourteenth-century misericords—even the first American bible. It stands in what was for years the capital of England, and the tombs of ancient kings can be found alongside those of more recent local figures such as Jane Austen.

Westminster Abbey, London. The ultimate receptacle of pageant and history in Britain, the setting of royal coronations, filled with tombs of Britain's great—including the Poets' Corner. The wonderful fan-vaulted ceiling in King Henry VII's chapel is worth a special visit.

Stately Homes

TO THE BRITISH, A MANSION IS not a mansion; with typical under-statement, it is a "stately home." Wherever you travel in Britain, you are rarely far from a stately home that is open to fee-paying members of the general public (see box). In southern England alone, any twenty-mile radius will usually yield at least one such home worthy of a visit.

It is only recently, however, that the general public has been allowed and encouraged to wander through what were once the grand and private homes of the British aristocracy. Times-have indeed changed. Well-trained staff, indispensable to the seamless upkeep of an elegant life-style, are hard to come by and de-manding of higher salaries than in the past. Many houses have suffered from the gradual selling off of sur-rounding lands, leaving insufficient acreage to farm and thereby support the main house. Those owners who lack the funds to keep up with the enormous maintenance costs on homes that may date back to medi-eval times, have found their difficul-ties compounded by death duties and property taxes.

Some owners have raised money by selling off prized and valuable items, forsaking hereditary luxuries for one more generation of privacy. Others, who have found that option unacceptable for whatever personal reasons, have opened their houses to the public. Many have signed them over to the National Trust of Great Britain, which renovates, maintains, and administers the property while allowing the family to continue living in some private part of the house. It's a mutually beneficial arrangement: the owner safeguards his heritage, and the public enjoys access to hith-erto exclusive surroundings. And, in many such cases, even the public areas maintain a lived-in atmosphere, with potpourri, fresh flowers, and family photographs set around the rooms. In spite of the inevitable velvet ropes and plastic runners, these homes are definitely *not* museums.

A visit to a stately home is far more than a chance to observe fine architecture and interiors; it is a rare opportunity to experience the flavor of a way of life largely lost to time. The owners of Britain's stately homes once were the nation's proudest pa-trons of contemporary art and archi-tecture, and their homes reflect their interests. Fine rooms lavishly adorned with paintings, priceless fur-niture, tapestries, rugs, silver, clocks, trinkets—many with their own quirky histories—are the result of genera-tions of serious collecting.

Stories of a particular family's for-tunes or misfortunes, eccentricities, scandals, and, of course, ancestral ghosts, add intrigue to the history of a home. But many owners of stately homes now recognize that history and intrigue alone won't attract visi-tors in the necessary droves. A num-ber of homes are now becoming, in various ways, historic amusement parks. In the mid-1960s, for example, the Marquess of Bath established a

BTA

The State Dining Room of Chatsworth House (above left) in Derbyshire displays an opulence in keeping with its seventeenth-century origins as the ancestral home of the Duke and Duchess of Devonshire.

Castle Howard (left and above) in North Yorkshire remains the ancestral home of the Howard family, descendants of Charles Howard, third earl of Carlisle, for whom it was built in the eighteenth century.

safari park on the grounds of Longleat House, where lions and hippos now complement the gracious Elizabethan façade of the family manse. At Blenheim Palace, visitors can now see not only the room in which Sir Winston Churchill was born, but also enjoy a collection of four thousand model soldiers, a narrow-gauge steam railway, and boat trips on the adjacent lake. Even the more "run-of-the-mill" stately homes offer detailed guidebooks, tour guides, tea rooms, and gift shops.

Most stately home inheritors remain steadfastly proud of their heritage and preserve and protect it. One owner places a large sprig of holly on the seat of each delicate chair on display—prickly dissuasion to footsore visitors. It's a neat metaphor for the combination of charm and sufferance that allows us to enter Britain's stately homes.

The Ten Best Stately Homes

1. **Beaulieu Abbey and Palace House**, near Lyndhurst, Hampshire. Buildings date from the thirteenth to the sixteenth centuries. Houses a celebrated collection of vintage motor cars and motorcycles.

2. **Blenheim Palace**, Woodstock, Oxfordshire. A huge eighteenth-century mansion by Vanbrugh, with landscaped gardens. Sir Winston Churchill's birthplace, it offers memorabilia, model soldiers, and railway and boat trips.

3. **Blickling Hall**, near Aylsham, Norfolk. A Jacobean house with formal gardens and an orangery.

4. **Castle Howard**, near York. An enormous eighteenth-century mansion by Vanbrugh; famous as the setting for the television series "Brideshead Revisited."

5. **Chastleton House**, near Chipping Norton, Oxfordshire. An unspoilt example of a seventeenth-century mansion. Eccentric, haunting, and crumbling.

6. **Chatsworth**, near Bakewell, Derbyshire. A fine seventeenth-century classical mansion. Ancestral home of the Dukes of Devonshire. Fascinating water gardens.

7. **Knole**, near Sevenoaks, Kent. One of the largest and most famous private houses in Britain, a seventeenth-century building with fifteenth-century origins. Possesses a large walled garden and "wilderness" lands.

8. **Longleat House**, near Warminster, Wiltshire. An important Elizabethan house built in Renaissance style; has landscaped gardens and a famous safari park.

9. **Stourhead**, near Frome, Wiltshire. A Palladian House begun in 1722, with famous landscaped gardens.

10. **Woburn Abbey**, near Dunstable, Bedfordshire. The eighteenth-century seat of the Dukes of Bedford. Offers a superb collection of paintings, *and* deer and safari parks.

Cottages: Life on a Human Scale

WITH ITS THATCHED ROOF, MEL-low stone walls, little lattice windows, and, of course, roses 'round the door, the English country cottage is everyone's fantasy of coziness, peacefulness, and comfort. Yet throughout Britain this idyllic scene is, in fact, a reality. Up and down the nation, you can still find villages where charming cottages cluster around the green, watched over by the church and amiably served by the village pub. The economic realities of modern Britain may mean that villagers now depend upon nearby towns or cities for their shopping and their jobs, but apart from this shift of emphasis, cottage life today is not merely viable but, indeed, flourishing.

This is living on a human scale. Small windows and thick walls make for good insulation, and with their low-beamed ceilings the rooms are easy to heat. A rebirth in the enthusiasm for traditional cottage gardening has seen cottage walls throughout Britain clad anew in honeysuckle (not to mention the inevitable sweet-smelling roses). Hollyhocks stand guard at small front doors, and paths leading to them are fringed with clove-scented pinks, bushes of lavender, the whiskered faces of violas, and sky-blue forget-me-nots. In back-yards, herbs, fruits, and vegetables are grown, making the cottage garden a fine blend of the romantic and the practical.

Britain is rich in good building stone, and the solid craftsmanship of local quarrymen and builders, especially in the seventeenth and eighteenth centuries, has resulted in thousands of cottages surviving the intervening years intact. Stone was cumbersome and costly to move in those days, and all local building was done with local materials. What with their lack of straight lines or true right angles and their typically rounded edges, British cottages really do seem to have grown naturally out of the surrounding countryside.

Look at a cottage and you see the very character, the colors and textures, of its regional landscape. There is stern-faced gray granite in the North; red, brown, and yellow sandstone in the Midlands; and creamy limestone and chalk in the South. In East Anglia, bricks are the primary building material, and cottages there are often decorated with bands and blocks of local flints, sometimes in a pretty checkerboard pattern.

Many cottages in Kent and Sussex are wooden, their walls hung with white weatherboarding. A wide variety throughout Britain are built of

Weidenfeld Archive

Tara Heinemann

Weidenfeld Archive

Charm, comfort, and harmony with nature typify English cottages. Many in western England, like the one at left in Bibury, Gloucestershire, are made from the local limestone. The "Christmas Tree Cottage" strikes a whimsical air (below), but often a lush garden, a thatched roof, and a cat provide just the right homey touch (far left).

frames of sturdy oak timbers and filled in with stone, brick, or wattle and daub (bundled reeds and mud). In Devon and Dorset cottages are made of cob, a very basic mixture of mud packed solid and mixed with lime to harden it. A local saying has it that as long as a cob cottage has "a good hat and a good pair of shoes"—that is, a roof to keep out the rain and a solid foundation—it will last for centuries. Painted pink, blue, or buff, cob cottages stand like

colorful blossoms amid the lush greenery of the West Country.

Cottage roofs are as varied as their walls, and may be finished in slate, terracotta pantiles, or wooden shingles. But the most famous cottage roofing material of all is thatch, tight bundles of reed, straw, or heather. Its multiple layers make for wonderful insulation, and a thatched house is warm in winter and wonderfully cool in summer. A good thatched roof will last as long as a

hundred years (provided care is taken that it doesn't catch fire!), and the demand for them ensures that the country art of thatching will continue to thrive in Britain.

Indeed, cottages are still perfectly sensible homes for thousands of working people—from fishermen's houses piled higgledy-piggledy on the steep slopes of the Cornish coast to the most windblown and isolated smallholder's dwelling in Northumbria. Yet when you look at the arche-

typal Cotswold cottage—tucked into the shelter of a vale, its honey-colored walls speckled with golden lichen—you still cannot help but be swept away by the romance of it all. The cottage itself reflects the seasons. In summer its garden will be crowded with bright flowers, and in winter the smoke will rise from its chimney into the damp chilly air. A powerful image of safety and well-being, this is a place we recognize in our hearts, wherever we come from.

SUNLIGHT ON FADED CHINTZ. THE gleam of country pottery on an antique Welsh dresser. The rich patina of a Hepplewhite table. A richly colored William Morris wallpaper. The crisp shadows cast by an Adam stucco ceiling.

There is a distinctive timelessness to British interior design in all its variety, a timelessness that is best ex-

dered bed-hangings, and grand oil paintings has its roots in the sixteenth century, a time when houses no longer had to double as fortresses. Windows grew larger (Hardwick Hall in Derbyshire, for example, was said to be "more glass than wall") and light flooded the interiors, demanding a playful new focus on decorative touches.

By the eighteenth century, comfort was, to a large extent, something taken for granted. Daybeds, richly upholstered chairs and sofas, thick carpets, and brocaded curtains were the prevailing styles of the day. During this period the interior decorator as we know him or her today first made an appearance in Britain, in the person of William Kent, an architect who

designed furniture for specific architectural schemes, such as his famous Double Cube Room at Wilton House in Wiltshire. His baroque style, owing much to European fashions of the time, gave great impetus to those who favored excess in their decor—not a particularly British trait.

More to the British liking of cool restraint was the work of the great

Interior Design: "The Quest for Comfort"

plained by the subtitle critic John Cornforth gave to his definitive book *English Interiors 1790–1840.* He referred to English interior design as "The Quest for Comfort"—something for which the British have always striven (with the exception, perhaps, of the denizens of the loftiest and draftiest palaces and stately homes).

To be sure, medieval British palaces, castles, and manor houses served more often as fortifications than homes. Floors were rush-covered, furniture was at a premium, and pictures and curtains nonexistent. It was design at its most functional. But one *could* say, without too much irony, that the look remains in high fashion today in many British city and country homes, where bare stone or brick walls are often the dominant decorative feature.

In contrast to such high minimalism, the British love of plaster ceilings, sculpted fireplaces, embroi-

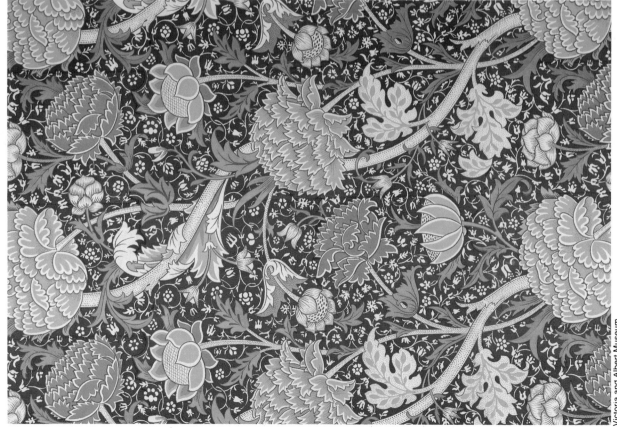

Victoria and Albert Museum

© Peter Paige

classical revivalists—Robert Adam in the late eighteenth century and James Wyatt in the early nineteenth. Both men undertook the obligatory Grand Tour of Europe, which played a significant part in the development of British taste. It was the custom at the time for aristocratic young men to complete their cultural education by traveling around the Continent, principally Italy, learning about (and plundering) "the Glory that was Greece, the Grandeur that was Rome." They liked what they saw. The Grand Tour left its mark on British homes of the period, from the grandest to the less grand, in the form of antique columns, busts, and garden ornaments, or skillfully executed interpretations thereof. Like Kent, Adam specialized in creating a *whole* look by matching walls, ceilings, curtains, and smaller objects—even designing a carpet pattern that cleverly mimicked a stucco ceiling.

As Mr. Cornforth's book points out, comfort in English interiors had been almost fully realized by 1840. Then came the Victorian era, a period of comfort carried to often tasteless excess. Rooms were overburdened with heavy hangings and rich upholstery, furniture so large as to be elephantine, and knick-knacks and pictures galore—a mishmash of styles swinging wildly from Byzantine to Renaissance. It took almost a century more for the stateliness and good taste of the Victorian era to be sorted out from the pedestrian and the bad, resulting in the Victorian revival interiors popular from the late

A wallpaper designed in the late nineteenth century by William Morris (left) typifies the craftsmanship and lush patterns for which he was noted. Interiors by David Hicks for the British Embassy in Washington, D.C. (above and right) combine traditional and antique pieces in a setting that nevertheless feels modern.

© Peter Paige

1930s to the present day (and exemplified in rooms designed by the late Sir Cecil Beaton).

The mass-produced and shoddy clutter of Victorian times *did* result in a number of worthwhile reactions to that predominant nineteenth-century style. William Morris in particular advocated a return to handmade "medievalism," which was most evident in his Red House in Kent. Reprints of Morris's beautifully pat-

terned wallpapers have been popular for decades. And the Art Nouveau movement, probably the only "genuine" style the late nineteenth century produced, offered another alternative to Victoriana. Harking back to the Regency period, rooms like those designed by the Scotsman Charles Rennie Mackintosh were treated as a decorative whole, with a cool, spare, wholly self-assured touch, which is his inimitable style.

In 1951, the Festival of Britain celebrated the latest and best in British design. But, to be honest, interiors shown at this much-needed postwar shot-in-the-arm to the country's morale were rather short on innovative style. It took interior decorators like John Fowler and David Hicks, in the mid-1950s, to pull Britain out of its war-induced drabness and introduce more color, texture, warmth, and, yes, comfort, to a public long starved of

Since the 1950s, Sir Terence Conran's Habitat stores have brought functional, attractive, and inexpensive modern design into ordinary British homes.

© Ken Kirkwood

In a dining room and sitting room designed by Laura Ashley (below and right), gently patterned prints and soft fabrics create a prototypical English country look.

Courtesy of Laura Ashley

Courtesy of Laura Ashley

such things. Even though Hicks, who now enjoys a worldwide reputation, designs mainly for the well-to-do, he created two important looks that have been adapted to the needs of the less-well-off: the use of good, modern pieces of furniture in old-fashioned settings and, conversely, the placing of old or antique furniture in a modern interior. If Hicks's interiors are sometimes too stylized (one feels that it would be a sin to move a vase one inch out of place), they nevertheless vibrate with color, imagination, dramatic contrast, and even wit.

Also world-famous, Sir Terence Conran's Habitat stores (known in America as Conran's) constituted another 1950s revolution in interiors. Conran brought comparatively cheap, well-designed, mainly wood furniture (in the prevailing Scandinavian idiom) and interiors to Britons and people worldwide who wanted the feel of a "modern" interior that was still comfortable and very affordable.

The 1950s saw the development of yet another significant influence in British interior design. The "country" look of the late Laura Ashley's designs did as much for interiors as it did for women's fashions. Sprigged prints and paisley patterns in soft colors and fabrics added up to a romanticized "old-fashioned" rural British style that probably never really existed. Yet it touched, and continues to touch, that love of nostalgia—and comfort—so dear to every loyal and sentimental British heart.

Chapter 3
Gardens

Public Parks and Gardens

London is blessed with a wealth of public parks. Hyde Park (below), in central London, offers woods, meadows, and a lake. The gates of Green Park (below right) recall its royal origins.

THROUGHOUT BRITAIN HUNDREDS of public parks and gardens offer city and country dwellers alike the chance to share the beauties of nature as presented through the gardener's art. And not surprisingly, these idyllic retreats for the populace are a legacy of the British aristocracy.

The term *park* originally referred to a tract of land set aside by the upper classes for hunting. The term was broadened in the eighteenth century to mean the lands adjacent to a gentleman's house—lands that were molded and embellished upon by garden designers of the so-called English Landscape School. While many such parks remain in private hands, others have been made accessible to the public over the years—having been deeded to the National Trust of Great Britain along with the stately homes they surround, or, as is the case with the Royal Parks in London, simply turned over to public use. Sections of Regent's Park were thrown open as early as 1841 and Hyde Park was made public by 1861.

In the nineteenth century, public parks became a feature of British urban life for the first time. Such parks were developed largely out of the Victorians' concern for reform, a concern that was goaded by the frequently appalling living conditions of the many citizens who had been

BTA

Every year, more private parks become public. Sheffield Park (right) in Sussex, with its magnificent landscape by Capability Brown, was acquired by the National Trust in 1954.

Weidenfeld Archive

drawn to urban centers by the Industrial Revolution. In effect, parks were seen as an opportunity for them to return, if only for a brief while, to nature. Charles Dickens in particular served through his novels to educate the public to the dreadful standards of living in London's East End. Soon, new London urban development schemes included parklands.

The tragedy of World War I led, paradoxically, to the growth of more public parklands. Vastly diminished numbers of men returned from the trenches, and suddenly the cheap labor upon which the owners of great private gardens had relied was no longer to be found. Grander, larger gardens were forced to economize and reduce their acreage, and a new trend of designating private gardens as public began. Many of the new gardens designed in the years after the war were specifically dedicated to the memory of the war dead.

In more recent years, the British government has come to look upon all of Britain as, in a sense, a public garden. Regions like Snowdonia in north Wales have been designated "areas of outstanding natural beauty," and are now under the protection of the national parks system. Combined with the efforts of the National Trust, vast areas of Britain are now being managed and preserved.

BTA

THROUGHOUT BRITAIN, MANY stately homes are wedded to gardens that match the splendor of their architecture and interior design. Thanks to the graciousness of their owners, some of the finest private gardens in Britain are now open to the public.

What one sees upon visiting these gardens can most frequently carefully chosen and tended plants.

On the other hand, one can view many private gardens that exemplify the unique natural garden traditions of the eighteenth century. Perhaps the finest example may be found at Stourhead in Wiltshire, where a gathering of temples, grottoes, Gothic cottages, and follies is surrounded by an outstanding collection of trees works of art using plants as their medium. Beyond the basic styles, you'll find dozens of flights of fancy throughout Britain: Moghul gardens (Sezincote), Japanese (Tatton Park in Cheshire; Newstead Abbey in Nottinghamshire), tropical (Tresco and Inverewe), and so on.

Surprisingly, many private gardens still remain private. But their owners often graciously open their gates periodically to the public, with the purpose of raising money for charity. By referring to the well-known "yellow book" of the National Gardens Scheme, one can follow, month by month and county by county, which private gardens are briefly opening to allow the public a taste of a leisured life set amidst rural beauty.

Great Private Gardens

be traced back to one of two broad traditions in garden design. The first is that of the classic formal garden, often Mediterranean in origin. One sees this kind of influence in the garden at Hidcote Manor in Gloucestershire, where strictly formal layout designs are softened by the informality of the planting schemes: tightly enclosed gardens near the manor house gradually give way to the carefully designed "natural" informality of streams and woodlands. Another outstanding example can be found at Sissinghurst Castle in Kent, where the poet and novelist Vita Sackville-West and her husband, the novelist Harold Nicolson, together created a six-acre garden in the 1930s that Sackville-West once described as a grouping of "outdoor rooms," interconnected in such a way as to give a delightful series of miniature romantic vistas. Another sort of classicism can be seen in the famous terraces and hanging gardens of Powys Castle in Wales, four steeply sloped levels of terrace walks with balustrades, statues, yew hedges, pear trees, roses, clematis, and dozens of other and shrubs, each carefully planted to create the effect of a natural woodland setting.

Within these broad traditional approaches, there are many permutations and variations, and many famous gardens contain elements of both. At Knightshayes Court in Devon, Sir John Heathcoat-Amory, grandson of the home's original builder, and his wife set out after World War II to create a garden on the mansion grounds; their remarkable creation includes a "garden-in-the-wood" filled with flowers, bulbs, and shrubs beneath a canopy of trees; a pool garden with statuary; a formal paved garden; and a willow garden. At Bodnant in North Wales, formal terraces offering magnificent views of Snowdonia National Park descend to a wild dell that includes some of the best groupings of azaleas, camellias, magnolias, and rhododendrons to be seen anywhere in Britain's rich gardening landscape.

Such elaborate gardens are, naturally, evocative of an age past, when a leisured class enjoyed an *embaras de richesse* and could create living

Many private gardens are now open to public view. The magnificent walled gardens at Hidcote Manor (below left) were begun only in 1905. The eighteenth-century landscape gardens at Stourhead are graced with Greek and Roman follies (left). Powys Castle in Wales (below) is famed for its terraced gardens.

THE ENGLISH, IT HAS BEEN SAID, are a nation of gardeners—and it is probably only because of the limitations of climate and topography that the saying has not been applied to the British people as a whole. As the aristocracy has designed and created its great gardens over the centuries, so have the common people of Britain developed a tradition of cottage gardening.

For generations, most cottage gardeners probably grew only herbs, primarily for medicinal and culinary use in the home. They would most certainly have had fruit trees—sharing valuable and limited garden space with a pig and, if time allowed, some simple vegetables. Any sense of giving those rudimentary gardens a decorative dimension was clearly secondary; first came the contribution they made to a fairly crude subsistence and survival.

The same mania for things horticultural that affected wealthy Britons in the nineteenth century seeped down through the social stratum of an emerging middle class to the average country cottage dweller (as well as to his urban-dwelling counterpart). A passion for vegetable growing welled up in the heart of the com-

A Nation of Gardeners

Weidenfeld Archive

mon British countryman, and the urge for excellence in home-grown produce was fueled by local village shows. And the town dweller, though he may have had only a paved yard adjacent to his urban abode, could lease a small patch of land, perhaps little more than ten by twenty feet, on the perimeter of town—an "allotment" for gardening. Indeed, the austere years during and following both world wars saw allotments become an important part of the lives of many Britons; and though they declined in the 1960s, allotments are at a premium again with the recent trend toward self-sufficiency.

Weidenfeld Archive

Tara Heinemann

It is in their gardens that Britons most openly show their pride—and their celebrated eccentricity. Allotment leaseholders on urban outskirts seem to be in silent competition, trying to outdo workers on neighboring plots with neater rows of plants, more beautiful decorative flowers, more splendid storage huts. A London suburbanite may spend every available hour rolling, fertilizing, watering, and weeding his little patch of lawn to give it the deep emerald velvet finish of a bowling green—no matter that it serves him no discernible practical purpose. In the same vein, an office worker will carefully tend an ever-growing collection of rare scented geraniums on the windowsill above her desk. Residents of the Findhorn religious commune in Scotland take special pride in the gargantuan fruits and vegetables they produce with the aid of the intense spiritual energy they transmit to the plants. And even the city apartment-dweller with no land at all will lovingly cultivate a windowbox for its springtime burst of brilliant yellow daffodils. If Britain, with all its natural beauty, may be thought of as a vast garden, then every Briton considers part of that garden—however small—his or her birthright.

Virtually any Briton with a patch of land to call his or her own will strive to make something grow there—and grow gloriously. This cottage garden overflows with foxglove and roses (far left), offering every room a view of something beautiful, while potted plants, hedges, and carefully tended beds (above center) provide nature with the requisite sense of order. Doorways may be flanked by clematis, which is sometimes trained to provide a natural frame (above).

The Chelsea Flower Show

THE HIGH POINT OF BRITAIN'S gardening calendar takes place over five festive days each May, when the nation's—perhaps the world's—most famous flower show blossoms on the grounds of London's Royal Hospital in Chelsea. For sheer size, splendor, and diversity of exhibits, few such international events rival the Chelsea Flower Show. Sponsored by the Royal Horticultural Society (RHS), the show draws upward of a quarter of a million garden lovers—an average of some seventy thousand people a day—from all over Britain and overseas. They converge on Chelsea by car, coach, bus, underground railway, and on foot, to marvel at the best of the blooms and the newest developments in horticulture and floriculture.

Traditionally (at least since 1913, when the first of the Chelsea shows was organized), Monday is devoted to the judging of exhibits and an afternoon visit by members of the Royal Family. Tuesday is officially the first day of the show and is reserved for RHS members. On Wednesday, Thursday, and Friday, the show is open to the general public. What confronts them as they eagerly troop into the Royal Hospital grounds is the largest canvas canopy in the world, which covers three-and-a-half acres and takes two dozen men more than a fortnight to erect.

Beneath the canopy's light and airy cloth stretches a dazzling panorama of flower and plant displays, separated by a grid of gangways in which one-way, no-entry, and no-turn directional signs maintain an admirably British sense of order and keep the human traffic flowing smoothly. A heady perfume thickens the air at this extravaganza, and the eyes are overcome by a visual assault of colorful vegetation. The exhibits themselves are microcosms of the planet's flora: alpine and rock garden plants, African violets, begonias, bamboo, cacti and succulents, daffodils, Iceland poppies, lilies, orchids, roses, sweet peas, and wildflowers. The gnarled miniature bonsai trees always collect a knot of fascinated visitors, as do the somewhat chilling carnivorous pitcher plants and Venus flytraps. Japanese flower arrangements, seven-foot delphiniums, and luscious displays of fruits and vegetables add extra sparkle to the show.

Not only nurserymen and professional growers exhibit; scientific and educational institutes and associations—including the Royal Botanic Gardens from Kew, the Society of Floristry, and the National Vegetable Research Station—also have stands, providing the public with information on their activities. Chief among those dispensing gardening wisdom are the staff from the RHS's own gardens at Wisley in Surrey.

For the crowds weaving along the avenues and paths surrounding the canopy, trade stands display, advertise, and sometimes sell a vast range of garden-related equipment and sundries—from wheelbarrows, fences, and fungicides to pruning tools, greenhouses, and spraying ma-

Harry Smith Collection

Harry Smith Collection

chines. Not everybody might want an herbal pillow, an aerobic compost maker, or a sundial, but all are available should the need exist. For those seeking new ideas in garden layouts and design, the open-air gardens invariably offer something to delight or stir the imagination. Garden exhibitors include individuals, colleges, businesses, and daily newspapers, and the themes they choose are wide-ranging and fairly self-explanatory: "A Topiary Garden," perhaps, or a "Suburban Sanctuary," or "A Bamboo Garden." The quality of design is high and some garden-scapes have had a striking influence on contemporary garden styles.

So much constant walking and standing can be extremely tiring, so several catering tents provide seating along with bracing cups of tea and other refreshments. In the nearby Ranelagh Gardens, visitors can stroll amid the trees and bushes or sit and listen to music from the bandstand, played by the Grenadier Guards.

By Friday afternoon, with the show about to end, the exhibitors are preparing to clean up and clear out. But one major event remains. At five o'clock, many of the plants are sold to the visiting public. A starter's bell signals a wild and chaotic rush for prized blooms, flowering shrubs, and potted saplings that seem too cumbersome to carry away. Five days of restraint have drawn to a close, and the Chelsea Flower Show finally lets down its petaled hair.

The annual Chelsea Flower Show in London is the most exuberant event in the British gardening calendar. Beneath the show's giant tent, exhibitors spare no expense nor effort in showing off their horticultural skills—whether they extravagantly create a giant topiary castle (left) or more straightforwardly produce an expanse of luxuriant blooms (above). Spectators, meanwhile, join in the show's spirit, even going so far as to don period costume for strolling among the exhibits (right).

Harry Smith Collection

Chapter 4
Food and Drink

Public Houses

PUBLIC HOUSES, MORE COMMONLY known as "pubs," are the undisputed social hubs of Great Britain. Virtually every block and alleyway in the nation's cities has one, often placed strategically on the corner, and it is there that office workers meet for a lunchtime or after-work drink and neighborhood residents meet for an evening's relaxation at their "local." Even the tiniest country village has its pub, where pints of beer and hearty meals are shared along with the local news and gossip from the neighborhood.

You can spot a pub easily enough by its sign. Pub signs have become one of the most popular forms of folk art in Britain. Their origins date back to a time when few Britons were literate, and every business was marked by its symbol as well as its name. Pub names are chosen as much—if not more—for their illustrative potential as for their appropriateness. To be sure, there are drinking themes: the Brewers Arms, the Leather Bottle, the Flask, the Punch Bowl, the Bunch of Grapes. But equally popular subjects include country concerns (the Plough, the Wheatsheaf, the Fox & Hounds, the Pack Horse, the Cherry Tree); royalty and the aristocracy (the Kings Head, the Prince of Wales, the Wellington, the George and Dragon); celebrities and famous characters (the Sherlock Holmes, the Samuel Pepys, the Charles Dickens); professions (the Dusty Miller, the Drummer Boy, the London Apprentice, the Cartoonist); and just plain whimsy (Ye Olde Cheshire Cheese, the Punch and Judy, the Mops and Brooms, the Who'd A Thot It).

Pubs are as varied as their signs, their locales, and the imaginations of their owners. Indeed, the 1960s in particular saw a rash of new or renovated pubs decorated with the most up-to-the-minute neon, plastic, and chrome—features as conducive to warm camaraderie as a fist in the eye. Such ersatz pubs, fortunately, had no staying power. The pubs that last are warm, real, and comfortable, extensions, in effect, of their patrons' living rooms—literally, public houses.

Two styles in particular come to mind when one sets out to describe the typical pub. The country pub is closest to the hearts of Britons, with its wood paneling; leaded windows with small panes of frosted green, rose, and white glass; and solid tables, chairs, booths, and bar, all made of oak or mahogany. You'll find such country-style pubs in both rural and urban settings, though the definitive ones are those that predate Britain's urban growth: coaching inns or riverside taverns over four centuries old, their ceilings low with exposed beams, their ancient floors worn and

The publican (bottom left) at The George pub on Mortimer Street, near Oxford Circus in London, pulls a pint of real ale from one of many casks the pub has on tap in its cellar. Like almost all pubs, The George has a painted sign to go with its name—in this case, a depiction of St. George, patron saint of England (above). Such good, traditional pubs become historic establishments. Ye Olde Cheshire Cheese (right), a venerable establishment off Fleet Street in London, was a second home to the renowned eighteenth-century man of letters Dr. Johnson, and continues to offer refuge to modern British scribes.

BTA

undulating, their walls darkened by decades of smoke from cigarettes or fireplaces.

More elaborate, even glamorous, yet no less comfortable is the Victorian pub, a public house that takes its style from the decorative excesses of nineteenth-century Britain. Stained glass windows, elaborately etched mirrors, velvet brocade-covered walls, and gleaming brass railings and bar fixtures are the stuff of such pleasure palaces. But their primary purpose remains the same: to create an atmosphere in which good drink and conviviality reign supreme.

Contributing to the warm fraternity of pubs are food, games, and entertainment. Most pubs offer such standard snack fare as bangers (grilled sausages), Scotch eggs (hardboiled eggs covered in sausage meat and rolled in bread crumbs), simple sandwiches and meat pies, and a ploughman's lunch (cheese, bread, and pickles); some have daily specials and regularly offer full meals. Many establishments still have dart boards and domino sets, and, depending on where you travel in Britain, you may even find such old country amusements as skittles (the aim of which is to knock down tiny wooden pegs with a weight swung on a string) or "toad in the hole" (also the name of a traditional recipe, but in Sussex a game that involves tossing discs through a hole). Some pubs hold folk music evenings or sing-alongs; others, such as London's Kings Head or the Orange Tree in Richmond, Surrey, have converted back rooms into small theaters that offer dramatic productions.

Supreme though the British pub may reign, it does not go unregulated. Pubs throughout Britain are strictly licensed and may only open and sell alcohol during specific hours—usually from 11:00 A.M. to 3:00 P.M. and 5:30 P.M. to 11:00 P.M. on Mondays through Saturdays, and from noon to 2:00 P.M. and 7:00 P.M. to 10:30 P.M. on Sundays. (Hours are extended in certain boroughs on market days, or in certain areas where working men keep unusual schedules.) Some ten minutes before closing time, the publican will shout out above the din of conversation the call for final drinks: "Last orders!" And then, on the dot, he'll conclude service with a shout of "Time, gentlemen!" No amount of begging or pleading will produce another drop of drink from his taps. This is, after all, a British institution, and rules must be followed.

Real Beer

SOCIAL INSTITUTION THOUGH the British pub may be, the ultimate reputation of any pub is determined by the beer it serves. Whisky may rule in Scotland and cider may be a popular alternative in many parts of the west and south of England, but beer is and will remain the national drink of Great Britain.

When a Briton speaks of beer, he is not referring to the pale, fizzy drink beloved of Americans, the Frenchman's *bière,* the Dutchman's *pils,* or the German's *pilsener.* "That," he will tell you, "is what we call a lager—refreshing enough, but not really beer." Indeed, lager accounts for a paltry one-third of the beer consumed in Great Britain.

What *is* real beer to a Briton is a markedly different, though not unrelated, drink—namely, ale. The difference lies in the way the beer is produced. Old-fashioned brewing is done by a process known as "top fermentation," during which the beer is produced at natural, relatively high temperatures, and the yeasts in the beer rise to the top of the brewing vats as the fermentation progresses. Such beer, including British beer, is notable for its complex, often assertive taste—a taste best appreciated when the beer is drunk at its brewing temperature, that is, not chilled.

In the nineteenth century, however, Bavarian and Austrian brewers perfected a method of bottom fermentation at low temperatures, which produced a more stable if less complex brew. While the rest of the world's brewers hurried to adopt the more efficient bottom fermentation method, British pride ensured that no foreigners would tell them how to make their beer. Hence ale remained the preferred beer of Britain.

And pride is the reason British beer continues to flourish to this day. By the 1970s, six large brewing conglomerates had been formed in Great Britain, controlling more than forty of the nation's breweries. The trend among these giants was, understandably enough, to produce a stable, controllable, consistent product—achieved by filtering, pasteurizing, or chilling beer. But in the eyes of the serious British beer drinker, any one of those processes can destroy the essence of a beer. Real beer is a living thing, which continues to ferment in its cask or bottle, developing flavor right up to the very moment it is poured into a glass.

In the 1970s, a consumer movement known as CAMRA arose spontaneously in Britain, the letters in its name standing for the *Cam*paign for *R*eal *A*le, and its members vigorously supporting any brewery, large or small, that strove to produce live beer by the time-honored methods. Their efforts helped assure the success of the sixty or so small, independent breweries throughout Britain, many of which opened after CAMRA was formed, as well as the seventy-odd independent British breweries. Indeed, even the conglomerates are placing a greater emphasis on their own cask-conditioned, less predictable brews today.

Predictable, consistent beer is not something the British hold in high esteem. And why should they? As the English beer expert Michael Jackson so neatly puts it, "A beer, after all, can be consistently boring."

Young & Co's Brewery

Some British breweries still keep teams of stalwart horses to pull drays loaded with kegs of real beer (left), a traffic-stopping sight that evokes tradition and garners publicity.

At The King's Arms in Aylesbury, Buckinghamshire, a denizen hoists a pint of the local brew (above). Many old pubs like the Victorian-style World's End Distillery on the King's Road in Chelsea, London (right) have names that harken back to a time when many pubs brewed their own beers.

A Guide to British Beers

While *beer* or *ale* is the generic term for the British brew, there are several subgroups from which a pub's denizens may choose:

Mild. The weakest of the ales, either pale copper in color or a darker opaque brown, and slightly sweet in flavor.

Bitter. A stronger, drier beer with, as the name implies, a somewhat bitter edge. Those designated "Special" or "Best" are usually higher in alcohol content.

Brown Ale. A sweetish, dark, bottled beer.

"Winter" or Old Ale. A very strong, full-bodied bitter, often referred to as "barley wine" when served in bottles.

Stout. A strong, very dark, rich ale with a thick creamy head, best typified by Guinness (brewed in Britain as well as Ireland) and Mackeson.

Malt Whisky

WHAT A FINE BORDEAUX IS TO jug wine, a true Scottish malt whisky is to the blended whiskies drunk by most of the rest of the world. What the majority of people think of as whisky (the spelling without the *e* is used for Scottish and Canadian products; the spelling *whiskey* is Irish, American, Japanese, and so on) is a blended spirit made from several different sorts of grain, in some cases colored with caramel.

But not a true malt whisky (which the Scots *never* refer to as Scotch). Scottish malt is made exclusively from barley grains that have been malted (that is, sprouted) to produce an enzyme known as maltase, which turns the grain to sugar during the fermentation process. Once malted, the grain is dried in the centuries-old traditional way, over peat fires that impart a distinctively smoky flavor to the barley and to the finished drink. After mashing, fermentation, and a double-distillation process in copper stills, a process that takes about a week, the spirit is "cut" to the desired alcohol level with fresh spring or stream water and left to age in oak barrels—usually casks that have previously held Spanish sherry, thus imparting still more character. A minimum of three or as many as fifteen years or more will pass before the whisky is finally bottled and sold.

Whisky that is the product of a single distillery is known as "single malt" whisky, and there are close to a hundred such distilleries producing single malt in Scotland today. Each of

The Glenmorangie Distillery Co.

A single malt whisky—unblended malt whisky from a single distillery—is a rich, complex drink. Single malts vary with their region and maker, just like fine wines. Glenmorangie (left) is one of the many Highland Malts—that is, malt whiskys produced in the northern Highlands of Scotland. Bowmore (far right) is one of a handful of single malts produced on the Isle of Islay off the southwest coast of Scotland. All malt whiskies are distilled in giant, gleaming copper stills like the one at Bowmore (above right). Several different single malt whiskys are combined to make "vatted malts" like those produced by Dewar's (bottom right)—whiskys more balanced and less idiosyncratic than single malts.

BTA

these single malts is as unique and distinctive as a chateau-bottled wine, the result of the process by which it was made, the unique tastes of the people who made it, the water, the location of the distillery, and countless other minute influences. Malts are generally grouped into four regional categories, much as wines are

grouped by region. The largest and, for that reason, the most diverse category is Highland Malts, those whiskies produced in Scotland's northern Highlands. Their flavors vary widely, from light and delicate to rich and heavy, with all manner of subtleties in aroma, consistency, sharpness or mellowness, and so on. What all

have in common, though, is a reputation for quality. Some of the better-known labels include Cardhu, Glenfiddich, Glenlivet, Glenmorangie, Glenturret, Macallan, and Talisker.

The malts of the Lowlands tend to have a lesser reputation, largely attributable to the fact that this region is home to the major distillers of blended whisky. But distinctive single malts can still be had from a quartet of Lowland distillers: Auchentoshan, Bladnoch, Littlemill, and Rosebank. Few whiskies are now made in the Campbelltown region on the Mull of Kintyre in southwestern Scotland, but two distilleries—Glen Scotia and Sprinkbank—still produce single malts. And finally, there are the malts of the Isle of Islay off Scotland's southwest coast; these, including Laphroaig, Bruichladdich, and Bowmore, are distinctive spirits that play an essential part in blended whiskies.

Ah, those blended whiskies. It's not that they're a bad drink; they're just an experience only tenuously connected to that of a true malt. But if the distinctiveness of a single malt whisky is too much for you, if the task of sorting through dozens of them to find your favorite is just too daunting, if you want a balanced, more predictable whisky, then try what is known as a "vatted malt." These, at least, are blended exclusively from single malts—either different years from the same distillery or a selection of complementary malts from different sources. Some fine vatted malts are made by Buchanan's, Findlater's, Glencoe, Glen Drummond, and Dewar's. What you'll get, in effect, is malt whisky by committee—but a blue-ribbon committee, to be sure.

John Dewar & Sons Ltd.

BTA

Traditional Foods

BRITISH COOKING HAS BEEN getting a bad rap for far too long. Images of meats cooked until dry and juiceless, of vegetables boiled to death, of heavy puddings in dense pastry casings, leave many people with the idea that food in Britain is stodge, stodge, and still more stodge.

The problem is, for the visitor not strongly committed to seeking out good food, British cooking *can* be appallingly tasteless and unimaginative. Average restaurant standards are not terribly high, and many tourists find that the daily special they ordered—whatever it might be called—arrives as a gray, unappetizing mess. (And, try though they might, no Briton has yet been able to make a sandwich that could be judged decent by North American standards, regardless of the fact that the sandwich was invented by an Englishman, the Earl of Sandwich.)

But *look* for good food in Britain and you will find it—in abundance.

Indeed, abundance is the operative word, for the best traditional British cooking speaks of heartiness and generosity. Take, for example, two quintessential British dishes: steak and kidney pie, and roast beef with Yorkshire pudding. The former combines chunks of tender beef with finely diced pieces of rich kidney, stewed together in a thick gravy and topped with a flaky pastry crust (the same mixture is also cooked pudding-style, steamed inside a pastry wrapper). The latter pairs thick slabs of beef carved right off the rib with a crusty, baked egg-and-flour batter perfectly designed to sop up gravy. Both dishes convey one primal culinary message: feasting.

Modern British cities do indeed have their refined, world-class restaurants full of *haute* and *nouvelle* cuisine. But good *British* cooking is still a country matter, the food of the inn, the tavern, and the farmhouse. Try the standard "pub grub" offered in

many public houses and you'll find decent, simple fare. There are "bangers"—basic sausages, the contents of which will vary with the region—served, perhaps, with a steaming dollop of "mash," that is, mashed potatoes. There are "pasties" —turnovers filled with meat, potato, and onion, the time-honored lunch of

the Cornish miner. And there's the ploughman's lunch: bread, pickles, and mustard accompanying a wedge or two of some of Britain's outstanding regional cheeses—a sharp, aged Cheddar, perhaps, or a mild, tangy Welsh Caerphilly, a creamy Cheshire, a rich, yellow Double Gloucester, or a tangy blue-veined Stilton.

Heartiness characterizes the best of British cooking, from a roast beef elegantly served with Yorkshire pudding (left) to a "pub grub" lunch—a pint of beer and rolls filled with cold cuts (above).

Connoisseurs worldwide prize many regional British specialities—among them the tangy blue-veined Stilton cheese (right), with walnuts and apples, or the tender, exquisitely flavored Dover sole (far right).

Travel to Britain's different regions and you'll find extraordinary country cooking. The North is famed for the finest fish and chips (a national favorite), for dry-cured Cumberland hams, and for Lancashire hot pot (an oven-baked stew of mutton or lamb, onions, and potatoes). The Midlands takes pride in its hand-raised pork pies, its "faggots" (seasoned meatballs made of pork liver and cooked in gravy), its game and Christmas geese, gingerbread, and the jam tarts known locally as Bakewell puddings.

In the lands watered by the Thames River, roast duckling from Aylesbury is proudly served in addition to chunky Oxford-style marmalade and a Brown Windsor soup made with steak, vegetables, and sherry. East Anglia serves up Norfolk herrings, succulent Colchester oysters, salt beef and dumplings, and wonderful puddings and preserves made from its abundant summer fruits. The south of England has outstanding seafood, including Dover sole and Whitstable oysters. Seafood abounds in the West Country of Devon and Cornwall too, where you'll

find such unusual and imaginative native dishes as stargazy pie—a pie of tiny whole pilchards (sardine-like fish) baked with their heads poking out of the crust, gazing heavenward.

Scotland has its own distinctive cuisine. There's cock-a-leekie soup, a rich broth of chicken and leeks; Scotch broth, a hearty soup-stew of lamb, barley, dried peas, and fresh vegetables; and incomparable smoked Scotch salmon. Then there's the notorious Scottish national dish, the haggis, a sausage-like mixture of offal, oatmeal, onions, and seasonings, stuffed into a sheep's stomach and boiled. Though many are turned off even at the thought of such a concoction, Scots swear by it, believing, in the words of the great poet Robert Burns, that it is indeed the "Great chieftain o' the puddin'-race!"

Wales, too, has a cuisine some-

what apart, reflecting its Celtic origins. Leeks are not only the national symbol, they are the national vegetable and figure in many a soup and stew. You'll be served excellent Welsh lamb, a hearty meat-and-vegetable soup known as *cawl,* and the world-renowned dish of melted seasoned cheese on toast, Welsh rarebit. The Welsh also dote on laverbread—not really a bread, but a fine seaweed that is harvested, slowly cooked to the consistency of puréed spinach (which it looks like), mixed with oatmeal, and usually fried in bacon fat.

To be sure, there's many a traditional dish in Britain that will evaporate the appetite of the neophyte. But the nation's regional foods, lovingly preserved and enthusiastically savored by those who have grown up on them, are indisputably good, honest cooking.

Tea

TEA IS THE GREAT BRITISH panacea. Just woke up and want to get the fuzz out of your head? Have a nice cup of tea, dear. Arrived home after a long, hard journey? Here, let's get you a "cuppa" to take the chill off. Feel a cold coming on? Ooh, let's put some tea in you quick. Broken heart? Let me fix you a cup, then tell me all about it, luv. (Want a biscuit with that?)

Every Briton over the age of ten (an arbitrary age chosen by some statistician with, doubtless, good reason) drinks, on average, about fifteen hundred cups of tea each year, which translates into some four cups per day. That makes tea the leading national beverage; as much of it is drunk as coffee, beer (the leading alcoholic drink), and all other alcoholic and non-alcoholic beverages combined, excluding water. About a third of the world's annual tea exports (which total around 250 billion pounds) are Britain-bound, to be consumed as straight, pure varieties, or, more frequently, to be mixed into one of the many popular commercial teas or leading gourmet blends.

Of the latter, the two household favorites in Britain are English Breakfast Tea and Earl Grey. A blend of Northern Indian and Ceylonese teas, English Breakfast produces a bracing, full-flavored cup—just the thing to wake one up on a blustery morning. Earl Grey, on the other hand, is composed of Indian tea or an Indian-Chinese blend, delicately scented with bergamot (a rare citrus fruit

R. Twining & Company Ltd.

Afternoon tea is one of the great British meals, whether served at home with just a pot of tea and a sliced and buttered tea loaf (left) or in grand style at one of myriad tea rooms across the nation (far right). British tea drinkers have a wide choice of distinctive varieties and blends, as evidenced in the line-up below from the famous London food store Fortnum & Mason (whose coffees, too, seem to be given names more appropriate to blended teas).

whose precious oils are more commonly found in perfume bottles), and exhibits a fine gentility, making it a perfect tea for afternoon service. Both English Breakfast and Earl Grey are commonly served with a spot of milk—sugar optional, of course.

Preferred blends aside, it is what is served *with* tea that elevates this custom to high ceremony. Though tea first became fashionable in Britain during the seventeenth century with the marriage of the Infanta Catherine Braganza of Portugal—a dedicated tea drinker—to King Charles II, it was not until the nineteenth century that the custom of taking tea as the centerpiece of a late afternoon meal named after the beverage itself caught on. Among the genteel classes, it became the done thing to take a light repast of tea with pastries and delicate sandwiches at four P.M.—something to tide one over until the evening meal. (The working classes, meanwhile, came to refer to their evening meal itself as "tea.")

Afternoon tea remains today one of the most charming and widely practiced British customs, enjoyed at

tea shops, pastry shops, fine restaurants, and hotels throughout the nation. What one gets at tea depends largely on the kind of establishment in which one takes the tea, and on what part of the country one happens to be in. It can be as simple as a cup or pot of the brew and a few unadorned biscuits (what Americans call cookies). Scones—sweet little soda-leavened tea cakes, usually studded with raisins—are a standard feature, and the inclusion of jam and a bowl of whipped cream (which becomes rich, yellow, thick-yet-pourable "clotted cream" in Devon and Cornwall) with which to top them makes the occasion a "cream tea." Scots invariably serve thick, crisp shortbreads or the rich fruit loaf known as Dundee cake. In the North they might offer a slice of a sticky treacle-and-ginger tart known as parkin or mincemeat-filled Eccles cakes. You'll get thick, griddle-cooked pancake-like pikelets in the Midlands, and sweet cheese-filled Richmond Maids of Honour in Richmond and Kew, outside London. At a "high tea," you'll be overwhelmed by a wide selection

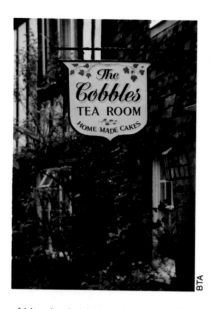

of biscuits, hot buttered scones with cream and jam, and assorted cakes and pastries—all preceded by delicate sandwiches of smoked salmon or salmon paste, cucumbers, watercress, and the like, cut into finger-sized pieces, the crusts trimmed.

When faced with such a feast, one finds it incredibly easy to understand and agree with the Mad Hatter in Lewis Carroll's *Alice in Wonderland*. In Britain, it is—or always should be—teatime.

Chapter 5
Literature

Poets Laureate

NOBODY KNOWS QUITE HOW THE custom arose, but since the thirteenth century, during the reign of King Henry III, Britain has had a royal poet or "Versificator Regis"—a man of letters officially appointed to compose verses commemorating royal or state occasions. Since the poet Geoffrey Chaucer assumed the position in 1389, Britain has had more than two dozen poets who have worn the metaphoric laurels of "Poet Laureate"—a continuous parade of literary talent (though sometimes lesser talent) spanning more than seven centuries.

Tradition is the bailiwick of the poet laureate and many men have won the position with their abilities to echo tradition rather than sound new voices in verse. Who today has heard of such poets as Samuel Daniel (appointed in 1599), Sir William D'Avenant (1637, and, incidentally, Shakespeare's godson—and, it has been suggested, his illegitimate son), Nahum Tate (1692), the Reverend Laurence Eusden (1718), Henry J. Pye (1790), or Alfred Austen (1896)? Yet all of these men, as well as their historical colleagues, enjoyed renown in their day as poets to the reigning king or queen.

Still in all, some remarkable poets have held the post of poet laureate. The first of these, and one of the greatest, was Chaucer, whose epic poem *The Canterbury Tales* offers a vivid picture of late medieval English life through the stories told by an oddly assorted group of pilgrims on their way to Canterbury. Chaucer's

Wearers of the laurels as royal poet have ranged from the likes of Geoffrey Chaucer (left) with his bawdy The Canterbury Tales *to William Wordsworth (above), the nineteenth-century poet who gloried in nature and Sir John Betjeman (right) whose verse was not, perhaps, deserving of critical acclaim, but was true to the spirit of the modern monarchy.*

The Mansell Collection Ltd.

The Mansell Collection Ltd.

Mark Gerson

he was a poet who was read and enjoyed widely, who loved his England, and who touched the roots of everyday British life with such gentleness and warmth that he was often, somewhat disparagingly, referred to as "the poet of the suburbs." One need only look at the titles of some of his poems to sense the man's common touch: "Inland Waterway," "In Willesden Churchyard," "Great Central Railway," "The Dear Old Village," and so on through more than fifty years of good-hearted, sometimes whimsical, always beautifully phrased and neatly rhymed verses.

Consider the final few lines of "A Ballad of the Investiture 1969," a sixty-eight-line poem Betjeman composed in honor of Prince Charles's investiture as Prince of Wales:

So we who watch the action
done—
A mother to her kneeling son
The Crown of office giving—
Can hardly tell, so rapt our gaze
Whether but seconds pass or days
Or in what age we're living.

You knelt a boy, you rose a man.
And thus your lonelier life began.

It's a nice piece, musical in sound, rapturously respectful of the British monarchy. Yet the lines also inject a more modern note, a sense of the bond between mother and son and of the awful burden being placed on the shoulders of a future king. In these and in many other lines, Betjeman was and is still regarded as a skillful writer of verse, an ardent monarchist, and very much a man of his time and place. And thus he was, and remains, a true British poet laureate to be remembered.

appointment as poet laureate made perfect sense. He was the son of a prosperous London wine merchant, and as a young man he served as a page in the home of the Countess of Ulster, daughter-in-law to King Edward III. He grew up to become a soldier and a scholar, a diplomat in the king's service, and Controller of the Customs in the port of London and Clerk of the King's Works in charge of a number of royal properties. Other great poets who have worn the laurels include Edmund Spenser (appointed in 1589), author of *The Faerie Queene*, an allegory glorifying England under the rule of Elizabeth I; the playwright Ben Jonson (1619); John Dryden (1670); William Wordsworth (1843); and Alfred, Lord Tennyson (1850).

Of the poets laureate in this century, surely the most beloved was the late Sir John Betjeman, who was appointed in 1972 and died in 1984. Sir John was no great poet for the ages, by any imaginative stretch, but

Other Tongues, Other Literatures

IT IS ALL TOO EASY TO FORGET that there are other languages besides English in Britain. Yet in northern Wales, the ancient language of Welsh is still the preferred tongue; and though Scotsmen as a whole speak English, their daily discourse, particularly in more remote parts of the country, is heavily steeped in native Scots. Both the Welsh and the Scots languages have rich literary heritages of their own, which have been cherished into the present day.

The most famous body of writing in Welsh literature is the collection of folk tales known as *The Mabinogion*. Having their genesis in ancient oral histories and legends, these stories were first written down almost a thousand years ago, and their current form is based on manuscripts dating from the fourteenth and fifteenth centuries. Included among them are a number of tales in which the legendary King Arthur appears, but the bulk of the stories focus on the birth, youth, marriage, adventures, and death of the Welsh hero Pryderi, son of Pwyll, Prince of Dyfed. These are dark, romantic, fantastical yarns, and some of their macabre power, surprisingly enough, was captured—if somewhat watered down and altered —in the animated Disney film *The Black Cauldron*.

National Portrait Gallery, London

Ask any Scot who the hero of Scottish literature is and you'll get just one answer: Robert Burns. The great Scots poet, who lived during the second half of the eighteenth century, wrote primarily in English, but his verses roll and sing with the Scots dialect. As well as publishing his own poetry, Burns traveled ardently throughout his country, collecting and writing down the lyrics to hundreds of old Scottish folk tunes and adding to them many of his own. When we join arms and sing "Auld Lang Syne" each New Year's Eve, we're singing a Robert Burns lyric. But Burns is, perhaps, at his best when he writes a love lyric whose images intertwine with the poet's clear love of his native land, as in "The Banks o' Doon":

> Ye banks and braes o' bonie
>   Doon,
>   How can ye bloom sae fresh
>   and fair?
> How can ye chant, ye little birds,
>   And I sae weary fu' o' care!
> Thou'll break my heart, thou
>   warbling bird,
>   That wantons thro' the
>   flowering thorn:
> Thou minds me o' departed joys,
>   Departed never to return.

Mary Evans Picture Library

Aft hae I rov'd by bonie Doon,
　　To see the rose and woodbine
　　　　twine:
And ilka bird sang o' its luve,
　　And fondly sae did I o' mine.
Wi' lightsome heart I pu'd a rose,
　　Fu' sweet upon its thorny tree!
And my fause luver staw my rose,
　　But ah! he left the thorn wi' me.

So beloved is Burns by his fellow Scots that his birthday, January 25, is the occasion for one of Scotland's grandest traditional celebrations, called simply "Burns Night." It is the occasion for readings of the poet's works, and grand feasting on boiled haggis (a sausage-like mixture stuffed into a sheep's stomach), "bashed neeps" (mashed rutabagas), and much fine whisky. Greater love has no nation shown for its finest poet.

The verses of Scottish poet Robert Burns (left) inspired illustrations by many artists of his time. In "The Cotter's Saturday Night," Burns depicted the close family life of a cotter—a cottage-dwelling farmer (above). "The Lass of Ballochmyle" (right), like many of Burns's poems, evoked the romance of the Highlands and its people.

Mary Evans Picture Library

Charles Dickens

IT IS ALL TOO EASY TO DISMISS Charles Dickens as a popular spinner of tales who stretched his novels out to fill twenty or more monthly installments in the popular Victorian magazines in which they first appeared. But no novelist before or since has so vividly recorded an entire world as Dickens did Victorian London. And no one has so captivated the imagination of the general reading public or won—at least posthumously—the admiration of the literary critical establishment.

Dickens literally has something to offer to everyone. A superb story-teller, he grips readers from first word to last: Who can forget the chase of Bill Sikes through the backstreets of London in *Oliver Twist*, or the stirring pageant of the French revolution in *A Tale of Two Cities*? A writer with a keen eye for the comic side of life, he created such warmly humorous characters as Sam Weller in the *Pickwick Papers* and the lunatic Mr. Dick in *David Copperfield*. A truly sappy romantic and sentimentalist, he loved happy endings and gave us the true love of Nicholas Nickleby for Madeline Bray, as well as poor little crippled Tiny Tim's merry Christmas in *A Christmas Carol*. A moralist, he also offered up satisfyingly wicked villains —including the wretched thief Fagin in *Oliver Twist*-and the entirely reprehensible schoolmaster Wackford Squeers in *Nicholas Nickleby*. A social campaigner, Dickens railed in all his works against the oppression,

©Mrs. Barbara Edwards/Mary Evans Picture Library

No tale of Dickens is more loved than A Christmas Carol *(left), in which miserly old Ebenezer Scrooge is visited on Christmas Eve by a succession of ghosts who teach him the true meaning of the season.*

The curio shop that gave its name to a Dickens novel (below) still stands in London not far from one of the author's homes. Dickens was at the height of success when this portrait of him with his daughters (right) was painted.

poverty, and suffering caused in particular by the British class system and the Industrial Revolution in Victorian Britain and in general by man's inhumanity to man.

Offering, as Dickens's novels do, so very much to delight readers, so much for us to savor, it's natural that even today he is still the most widely loved British writer. Teeming with life, his novels continue to live on. The humor remains fresh, the characters (many of them dazzling caricatures of Victorian English types) are still sharply etched, the stories exciting,

and the lessons to be learned deeply touching and true.

No wonder, then, that Dickens's works have been adapted to other media that extend their impact, allowing his stories to reach those who might be reluctant to pick up a book in excess of six hundred pages. Most of his novels have been brought to the large or small screen. Theater audiences have enjoyed such stage musicals as *Pickwick*, *Oliver!*, and, most recently, the hit Broadway version of the unfinished *The Mystery of Edwin Drood*.

But, without a doubt, the most definitive Dickens adaptation of the century was the Royal Shakespeare Company's eight-and-a-half-hour dramatization of *Nicholas Nickleby* in 1980. A cast of some two dozen actors portrayed *every single character* in Dickens's tale of the morally courageous young Nicholas and the downtrodden orphan boy Smike. And it was not the actors' skills alone—though they were abundantly apparent—that brought dozens of characters to life on-stage. What became clear was that these actors

were *inhabiting* roles so perfectly drawn by Dickens they could not help but have the ring of truth to them. Such truth drew the audience in, allowing them to lose themselves completely in the world of Victorian England. Raucous laughter, chilling terror, and heartfelt tears followed upon each other in close succession. It didn't matter that it was the stage rather than the printed page; the point is, the production was entirely faithful to the printed page. Once again, Charles Dickens had worked his masterly magic.

Children's Literature: A Little Girl, a Bunny, a Toad, and a Bear

FOUR OF BRITAIN'S MOST OUTstanding contributions to literature involve a naive little girl, an immature rabbit, an egotistical toad, and a brainless bear. Granted, they don't sound like a promising lineup, but in the hands of Lewis Carroll, Beatrix Potter, Kenneth Grahame, and A.A. Milne, respectively, Alice, Peter Rabbit, Mr. Toad (of Toad Hall, of course), and Winnie-the-Pooh became immortalized in fiction.

Lewis Carroll (the pseudonym of Charles Lutwidge Dodgson) broke fantastic new ground in children's literature with the publication in 1865 of *Alice's Adventures in Wonderland*, the tale of a young girl who follows a white rabbit down a rabbit hole and into a nonsensical world inhabited by characters such as the Mad Hatter, the Cheshire Cat (who could slowly disappear until only his grin remained), the March Hare, the Gryphon and Mock Turtle, and the Ugly Duchess. Such a tour de force of imagination was, surprisingly, the work of a relatively solitary lecturer in mathematics at Christ Church, Oxford. Young Alice Pleasance Liddell,

The Mansell Collection Ltd.

National Portrait Gallery, London

The adventures of Alice sprung from the mind of Charles Lutwidge Dodgson (above), who wrote under the name Lewis Carroll. The wildly imaginative tale grew even more vivid in Sir John Tenniel's depictions of such scenes as Alice's tea party with the Mad Hatter, the Dormouse, and the March Hare (left). Beatrix Potter's animal stories and illustrations have become nursery favorites, as much in demand on children's dishware and money boxes (right) as on the printed page.

Josiah Wedgwood & Sons Ltd.

the middle daughter of the dean of Christ Church, was Dodgson's inspiration for the tale, which he concocted to tell to the girls on a river outing in the summer of 1862, and then wrote out longhand—with his own simple, humorous illustrations included—as a Christmas present for Alice, and entitled *Alice's Adventures Under Ground*. An expanded version of the story came out three Christmases later, with pictures drawn by the great illustrator John Tenniel.

Young Alice's adventures were an early influence on the imagination of Helen Beatrix Potter, the London-born daughter of a well-to-do barrister.

Though she wanted for nothing materially, young Beatrix was deprived of the affection of her parents, and escaped into the worlds of reading and nature drawing. In 1893, at the age of twenty-seven, she wrote a letter to the five-year-old son of one of her former governesses, with words and pictures telling him a story featuring one of her pet rabbits, Peter, and his dangerous encounter in the garden of Mr. McGregor. Six years later, she was encouraged by a friend to publish privately an expanded version of the story, in an edition of two hundred fifty. This charming, innocent, beautifully illustrated tale met with huge

success, and the book was picked up and republished by the London firm of Frederick Warne & Co., which went on to publish more than two dozen of her little books—the first body of literature aimed expressly at very young readers.

The Scotsman Kenneth Grahame always dreamed of being a full-time man of letters. But real life got in the way and, instead of entering Oxford University and pursuing the academic life, his father obtained for him a clerkship in the Bank of England, where he started working in 1879, at twenty. Grahame was hugely successful there, becoming its secretary

Charles Scribner's Sons

The great illustrations of E.H. Shepard imprinted on young minds forever the exact *look of the characters in Kenneth Grahame's* The Wind in the Willows *and in the books of A.A. Milne (shown at right with his son, Christopher Robin). Shepard captured Toad's braggadocio (left), as well as the gentle charm of Pooh and his friends—images that have helped spawn a wide range of games, toys, and other paraphernalia (below).*

National Portrait Gallery, London

in 1898; and all the while, he wrote essays and stories about children. He had one child of his own, born in 1900, and on the night of his son's fourth birthday, Grahame lulled him to sleep by making up "stories about moles, giraffes & water-rats." Giraffes aside, this was the genesis of *The Wind in the Willows* (eventually published in 1908), a warmly evocative tale of the adventures of Mole, Water Rat, Badger, and the irrepressible Mr. Toad, and one steeped in a deep love of the English countryside surrounding the Thames River.

The countryside and stories told to a young boy also play a major role in *Winnie-the-Pooh* (published in 1926) and *The House at Pooh Corner* (1928), two books of stories suggested to A. A. Milne by his son Christopher Robin Milne's toy animals. Milne brought those animals to

life: Tigger, the rambunctious tiger forever pouncing; the ever-depressed Eeyore the donkey; the sweet, slightly wimpy (for some tastes, at least) Piglet; wise and crotchety old Owl; Kanga and her playful child Roo; and, of course, addleheaded, sweet-tempered Pooh, ever in search of a jar of honey. These vividly drawn characters (all the more vivid for the illustrations of the great E.H. Shepard) have a seemingly universal appeal that hasn't been tarnished by their recent transformation into bland cartoon characters with American voices at the hands of the Disney mouse factory.

Like all good literature, Pooh— along with Toad, Peter, and Alice— can take such popularizing abuse; they're good enough to stand above it, on their own, read and cherished by children and former children alike.

Fortnum and Mason PLC

Unconventional Sleuths

London Regional Transport

CONSIDER, IF YOU WILL, *THE ADventure of the Norwood Builder* by Sir Arthur Conan Doyle. A "wild-eyed and frantic young man, pale, dishevelled, and palpitating," bursts into the Baker Street quarters shared by Mr. Sherlock Holmes and John H. Watson, M.D. Gazing with unerring accuracy down the twin barrels of his infinitely aristocratic nose, Holmes addresses his visitor, who has introduced himself as one John Hector McFarlane. "You mentioned your name as if I should recognize it," says Holmes, "but I assure you that, beyond the obvious facts that you are a bachelor, a solicitor, a Freemason, and an asthmatic, I know nothing whatever about you."

They don't talk like *that* in the works of Raymond Chandler or George V. Higgins.

Ever since Sherlock Holmes sallied forth from 221b Baker Street in his cape and deerstalker, puffing at his foul-smelling meerschaum and chuntering on at the amiable but imbecilic Dr. Watson, the Great British Detective has cut a preposterous figure. While American crime fiction tends to make a virtue of the "procedural," in which a Watsonian logic, inexorably applied, triumphs in the end, British sleuths are, like Holmes, more likely to be monied amateurs with a strong line in legerdemain.

The Mansell Collection Ltd.

National Portrait Gallery, London

"A curious collection," says Dr. Watson as Sherlock Holmes examines the contents of a trunk in this illustration by Sidney Paget to The Musgrave Ritual *(left). Scenes from Holmes's cases now grace a tube station (above left) not far from his fictional home.*

A journalist, essayist, critic, novelist, and poet, G.K. Chesterton (above) is best known today for his short stories featuring Father Brown, a Catholic priest in a small East Anglian town who spends as much time solving crimes as saving souls.

Recently, one or two good British crime writers have made their heroes true professionals. John Le Carré's George Smiley of the innermost circles of Britain's secret service and P.D. James's Chief Inspector Adam Dalgliesh of Scotland Yard are two prime examples, though neither is what you might call conventional. Other popular modern detectives such as Simon Brett's Charles Paris or Tim Heald's Simon Bognor maintain the true Holmesian tradition— eccentric, amateur, irritating, and, perhaps most important of all, awkward. The true-blue British detective is a nonconformist who disdains authority, convention, and anyone at all who gets in his way.

Yet these sleuths often look conventional. It's a good cover. Lord Peter Wimsey, Dorothy L. Sayers's languid 1920s hero, kinsman of the Duke of Denver, Old Etonian and Balliol man, had all the Establishment attributes, including prowess at cricket. He also had a ludicrous turn of period phrase. ("That's torn it," he says as the car hits the ditch at the beginning of *The Nine Tailors*.) But he still had a sharp and unconventional forensic mind. G.K. Chesterton's Father Brown was a Roman Catholic priest, but with his penchant for detection he wasn't just any ordinary priest. And Margery Allingham's Campion is said to have been "hard to recollect and impossible to describe," even by those who knew him—something to do with his "vacuity of expression."

Agatha Christie, the best-known of all the great English mystery writers, plotted her stories brilliantly but wrote them abominably. Her Miss Marple is merely "that sweet old lady" (heh, heh!), though crime fiction chronicler Dilys Winn had a brilliant flash of intuition when she pondered what Miss Marple would be like if she had money and offered us a picture of Her Majesty the Queen Mother (an irresistible idea). Dame Agatha's Hercule Poirot is, of course, Belgian, and doesn't count.

In some respects, the perfect English sleuth is the famous Inspector Appleby, the creation of Michael Innes (pseudonym for the literary scholar J.I.M.—John Innes Mackintosh—Stewart). Appleby is best encountered in *Death at the President's Lodging*, set in 1936 at an Oxford College, which is an even better setting for English murder than the more popular country house. Appleby leaves Scotland Yard in swell style in "a great yellow Bentley" (even though he is a mere inspector) and is swiftly revealed as a prototypical combination: an "intensely taught product of modern police college" and something more "contemplative" and "tentative." These, speculates his creator, "were the tokens of some underlying, more liberal education . . . a schooled but still free intelligence."

Or, to put it another way, unorthodox and awkward. And also, like all the great British detectives, endowed with powers that are universally recognized as bordering on the miraculous, or perhaps, supernatural. For when the local plodding policeman greets Appleby in Oxford, he says, "It's a mystery right enough, Appleby. In other words, it looks like one of your cases, not mine."

Of course, it is mystery right enough for most of us. But for the British supersleuth, as always, it's elementary, my dear reader.

IT IS A GRUBBY LONDON THOR-oughfare that runs parallel to the River Thames between Ludgate Circus in the East and the Law Courts in the West. As a street, Fleet Street is nothing much to look at, but as a concept it generates as much myth as any road in town. It is called "the Street of Adventure," as well as "the Street of Ink" and "the Street of Shame." The *Oxford English Dictionary* describes it not as a street but

Fleet Street

as "the London press" or "London journalism," which gets to the heart of the matter.

In point of fact, only two of Britain's national newspapers have their main offices on Fleet Street itself. One is *The Telegraph*, whose building looks as if it had been designed by Mussolini in a state of depression. The other is *The Express*, whose shiny black-tiled façade reminds one of nothing so much as an enormous municipal lavatory. For years *The Times*, doyen of the British press, was just around the corner at Printing House Square, opposite Blackfriars Station, and recently *The Sun*, the popular daily with Britain's largest circulation, had been on Bouverie Street, a side street that runs south off Fleet Street itself. The last two papers, however, are owned by Australian-born newspaper baron Rupert Murdoch, and in January 1986 he summarily removed them to new quarters in the redevelopment zone of London's deserted docklands in Wapping, a complex the unions have

dubbed "Fortress Wapping." *The Telegraph*, recently acquired by Canadian millionaire Conrad Black, moved its own printing operation to the same docks in the autumn of that year, with *The Express* following in its wake. Fleet Street as the physical embodiment of British journalism is dying, dying, dead.

But British journalism goes on, inching ahead, albeit belatedly, into the twentieth century. The man who

precipitated the long overdue "technological revolution" in Fleet Street is Eddie Shah, who launched his brand-new, full-color, seven-day-a-week paper *Today* on March 4, 1986. Shah, who had cut his teeth on "giveaway" locals in the north of England, never went near Fleet Street with its antiquated machinery and restrictive union practices. Instead, he set up shop in Pimlico, a rather down-at-the-heel London neighborhood between Chelsea and Westminster, and proceeded to produce a newspaper that dramatically undercut the cover prices of his opposition.

Such competitive tactics now seem inevitable in a country with upward of eleven national daily newspapers and ten national Sundays. Britain's morning tabloid newspapers, such as *The Sun* and the *News of the World*, are little more than scandal sheets devoted to "exclusive" stories about television stars and risqué full-page photographs of generously endowed young ladies. But the circulation battle has recently spread to

The daily newspaper is an essential part of daily life for many Britons. For the businessman taking a break in St. James Park (left), the Financial Times with its distinctive pink-colored newsprint is as crucial to survival as a bowler hat and an umbrella.

Laurie Sparham/Network

Mike Abrahams/Network

The Express *newspapers are among the minority of papers with headquarters still on Fleet Street (left). Many papers are seeking ways to modernize and cut costs, and at the forefront is the full-color daily Today, launched in 1986, which offers state-of-the-art technology to journalists and production staff alike (above).*

even the old "quality" newspapers such as *The Times*, which has moved relentlessly down-market, going so far as to institute bingo-style competitions to woo new readers.

Yet, along with the left-wing *Guardian* and the *Financial Times*, *The Times* retains a world-class reputation for its comprehensive coverage of national and international affairs. And *The Times* still staidly maintains many of its traditions. Its daily crossword puzzle is known for maddeningly cryptic clues that turn thousands of devotees into code-breakers every morning. Its letters-to-the-editor page, aside from space for correspondence on serious issues, always saves room in the lower right-hand corner for more eccentric, some-

times pun-filled letters, including, each spring, a missive from some lucky bird-watching reader who has sighted the first cuckoo of the year.

Thanks to these traditions, along with the "tits and bum" pictures, the serious news, and the celebrity exclusives that the papers dish up every day, Britons remain among the world's most avid newspaper readers The morning newspaper habit is universal, as anyone who takes a rush-hour commuter train, tube, or bus can see. The Briton on his way to work may no longer wear a bowler hat or carry a tightly rolled umbrella, but he still hides behind his newspaper. Fleet Street, at least in its entrepreneurial spirit, lives on in the hands of Britain's voracious readers.

Chapter 6
Theater

Shakespeare's Legacy

THERE IS NO DISPUTING THE FACT that William Shakespeare was the world's greatest playwright, and Britain's greatest contribution to world theater and literature. One need only consider his output of thirty-eight plays (a number that includes his early uncredited apprentice work on *Henry VI, Part 1*, written in 1589–90, and his possible collaborations with John Fletcher on his two final plays, *Henry VIII* in 1612–13, and *The Two Noble Kinsmen*, 1613–14): historical plays such as *Richard III, Henry IV, Parts 1 and 2*, and *Henry V*; tragedies such as *Romeo and Juliet, Hamlet, Othello*, and *King Lear*; and comedies such as *The Taming of the Shrew, A Midsummer Night's Dream, Much Ado About Nothing, Twelfth Night*, and *All's Well That Ends Well*.

One need only think about the immortal characters he chronicled or created: the spiderlike, misshapen, and scheming King Richard III; power-hungry Lady Macbeth, driven mad by her misbegotten plottings; rollicking Sir John Falstaff, so popular in the Henry plays that public demand forced Shakespeare to write a play in which he starred, *The Merry Wives of Windsor*; Ophelia, driven to madness by Hamlet, serenely singing as she floats to her death; proud Brutus, falling on his sword with honor rather than face capture for the murder of Julius Caesar.

And then, of course, there are the sonnets, 154 fourteen-line poems that rank among the finest poetry ever written, including what is arguably the greatest love verse ever set to paper—the eighteenth sonnet, which begins,

> Shall I compare thee to a
>   summer's day?
> Thou are more lovely and more
>   temperate.

and ends,

> So long as men can breathe or
>   eyes can see,
> So long lives this, and this gives
>   life to thee.

But Shakespeare's importance to Britons and to all English-speaking peoples today is far more pervasive than most people realize. The fact is, though many people have seen his plays, many more have not and never will. Yet, Shakespeare's influence on the English language remains powerfully alive. When we say that a man driving a hard bargain wants his "pound of flesh," we are referring to *The Merchant of Venice*. When we say that "a rose by any other name would smell as sweet," we're quoting Juliet in the famous balcony scene. Jest at "what fools these mortals be," and you're scoffing with Puck in *A Midsummer Night's Dream*. Call an ardent lover a Romeo, an unscrupulous businessman a Shylock, and you're referring to Shakespearean characters. Say that "all the world's a stage, and all the men and women merely players," and you're in agreement with Jaques in *As You Like It*.

Shakespeare's creative power has left its stamp on the way we all express ourselves in English, and whether we know it or not, has added a little literature and poetry to all our lives.

Apart from his profound contributions to the English language and to world literature, Shakespeare's legacy also manifests itself in Britain in a much more tangible way—in the tourists it attracts and in the outstanding theater it inspires.

Shakespeare's birthplace, in the small country town of Stratford-upon-Avon, ninety-six miles northwest of

National Portrait Gallery, London

The stylistic interpretation of Shakespeare's plays has changed with time. This advertisement for a 1907 production of As You Like It (above) shows the trend in Edwardian England away from Elizabethan costume. Scholars have documented that the Henry VI plays were the first to be published by Shakespeare in the 1590s. The first complete collection of all his works, however, was published posthumously in 1623 in the Hemmings and Condell edition of the First Folio (above right).

London, has become a modern Mecca for tourists. But surprisingly, little attention was paid to the playwright's home town for the century and a half following his death in 1616. The first man to honor Stratford was the great seventeenth-century actor David Garrick, who organized an ill-fated, flood-wracked Shakespeare "Jubilee" in the town in September 1769. Oddly (but only so if one discount's Garrick's actor's ego), none of Shakespeare's plays were performed at the three-day festival, and only snippets of Shakespearean lines were quoted in the seemingly interminable odes Garrick declaimed to the great dramatist's memory.

Not until more than a century later was a theater dedicated to performing Shakespeare's plays built on the bank of the Avon, when the first Shakespeare Memorial Theatre opened on April 23, 1879 with a production of *Much Ado About Nothing*. This theater would become the seed from which would grow one of the world's greatest theater troupes—the Royal Shakespeare Company.

But, the RSC apart, Stratford itself today is a continuing Shakespearean show that entertains many more tourists than ever see one of his plays.

Remarkably, the town has changed little from Shakespeare's time—discounting, of course, the high street shops with their neon signs, the automobile traffic and the less-than-quaint modern garb of the local denizens. The point is, were he to return today, Shakespeare could still find his way around. There, on Henley Street, is the home where he was born. You can stroll along the country path to the neighboring village of Shottery, a mile away, where stands to this day the thatched cottage home of Anne Hathaway, Shakespeare's wife. Next to Holy Trinity Church, in which Shakespeare was baptized, is the graveyard where Shakespeare's tombstone stands, its inscription ending with a warning that "Curst be he that moves my bones." And, perhaps most significant of all, is the old stone bridge designed by Sir Hugh Clopton, which still arches over the Avon adjacent to the Royal Shakespeare Theatre. It was this bridge that Will Shakespeare, a young country man in his early twenties, crossed one day as he left his home of Stratford-upon-Avon and headed for London where, during the next twenty-some years, he would work as an actor and a playwright and achieve immortality.

The Great Theater Companies

THROUGHOUT BRITAIN, THE NAtion's centuries-old stage tradition is carried on in hundreds of theaters large and small, professional and amateur. But towering above all this activity are two of the world's greatest theater companies, both of them exemplars of the British art of acting and theatrical production: the Royal Shakespeare Company (generally known as the RSC) and the National Theatre of Great Britain (or the National). Both companies exist through government support—via the Arts Council of Great Britain—along with solid audience backing and, in recent years, with the Conservative Party's move away from state socialism, the assistance of corporate backers whose hard-business reputations are burnished by such worthy endeavors.

The RSC got its start with a short festival of Shakespeare's plays performed at his birthplace, Stratford-upon-Avon, in 1864. That was followed a decade later by a campaign to build a permanent theater there dedicated to the Bard's plays; the Shakespeare Memorial Theatre opened in 1879 with a performance of *Much Ado About Nothing.* Almost half a century of productions ensued, and a Royal Charter was granted to the theater in 1925—one year before it burnt to the ground. A new theater, which still stands, was opened in

Stratford on Shakespeare's birthday, April 23, in 1932, and became the home for a growing troupe of players "every member of which would be an essential part of a homogenous whole," as the company's director Sir Frank Benson said in 1905, "consecrated to the practice of the dramatic arts and especially to the representation of the plays of Shakespeare."

Peter (later, *Sir* Peter) Hall became the theater's director in 1960, at the time it officially became the RSC. Under Hall, and later Trevor Nunn, the company continued to grow, first adding in 1974 a small experimental space in Stratford called The Other Place, then two stages in the futuristic Barbican Centre in London in 1982, and most recently, in the sum-

mer of 1986, a fifth stage, The Swan, in Stratford, dedicated to plays by Shakespeare's contemporaries. Throughout its recent history, the RSC has toured its productions throughout Britain and the world, as well as preserved them on film, television, and records.

A similarly ambitious program is pursued on the National's three

Chris Davies/Network

Donald Cooper/London

BTA

Britain's great theater companies attract its finest actors, such as David Threlfall and Roger Rees in the RSC's Nicholas Nickleby *(left) and Ian McKellen in* Coriolanus *(above) at the National.*

In 1982, the RSC moved its London home from the antiquated Aldwych Theatre to an ultra-modern complex within the new Barbican development (above right) in the City of London.

stages in its modern concrete home along the South Bank of the Thames in London. The complex opened—under Peter Hall's direction—for its first performances in the spring of 1976, a century and a quarter after talks aimed at establishing a truly national theater company first began, and decades after a "National" company was performing classics at the Old Vic Theatre in London. On the South Bank, as at the RSC, one finds a permanent company of actors, directors, designers, and technicians who work together over the course of a year or more. Company members work together on many productions, which adds intensity and depth to their performances through a sense of common purpose.

Naturally, the two companies have their similarities and differences. The RSC's repertoire tends to be more classical and specifically Shakespearean, while the NT over the years has done more works by contemporary British playwrights; yet the NT does

its share of the Bard and other classics, and the RSC has premiered plays by Tom Stoppard and others, as well as such daring works as its sensational eight-and-a-half-hour adaptation of *Nicholas Nickleby.* At the RSC, one gets a stronger sense of truly classical acting, perhaps as a result of the intensive training company members get in speaking Shakespearean verse; while at the NT, styles seem more modern and a touch less uniform in approach. Nevertheless, many great actors have migrated from one company to the other, and often back again—among them Sir John Gielgud, John Wood, Michael Hordern, Ian McKellen, Albert Finney, and Derek Jacobi. What both companies have in common is the overriding goal of creating great theater worthy of the nation they represent—and, despite their differences and the occasional failures that inevitably occur on the cutting edge of the arts, both succeed mightily in achieving that goal.

Knights of the Stage

IN JAPAN, THE GOVERNMENT DE-clares its greatest craftsmen and artists to be "living natural treasures." The British bestow knighthoods on their home-grown treasures, and the most dazzling of the lot are surely the knights of the British stage. (Sad to say, there is no comparable mystique surrounding their female counterparts, despite that title's having been bestowed on such enchanting actresses as Peggy Ashcroft and Edith Evans.) And the three greatest theatrical knights of this century are indisputably Ralph Richardson, John Gielgud, and Laurence Olivier.

They are three very different ac-tors, indeed—different in looks, in personalities, in acting styles, and in the roles they've played. Yet all three have essential qualities in common: an excess of talent, a love of the stage and of theater, and an unstinting dedication to the art and the craft of acting—the ability to transform themselves into masterly instruments of the stage.

In fact, the musical metaphor is a tempting one to apply to these great actors. Ralph Richardson would have undoubtedly been something deep, mellow, slightly quirky—a cello, perhaps, or more likely a bassoon. He was a homely man with rounded, comical features, he excelled as a character actor, and early in his career earned a reputation as the embodiment of the common Englishman. Though he played many roles, both classical and modern, on stage and screen, his definitive portrayal was that of Sir John Falstaff in Shakespeare's *Henry IV, Parts 1 and 2* at the Old Vic in the 1944–45 season. Olivier paid him the highest accolade for that role: "I had always dreamt of his Falstaff," he wrote in his autobiography, "and he succeeded in bettering my wildest dreams."

John Gielgud is a flute—long and lean of body, fine featured (though possessing a truly beaklike nose), incomparably melodious of voice. Gielgud is the true British aristocrat, an actor who gave his generation not one or two but *four* different and definitive Hamlets—in 1930 at the Old Vic; 1934 at the New Theatre (directing himself); 1939 at Kronborg Castle, Elsinore, in Denmark; and 1946 at the Cairo Opera House. He was stylish perfection as John Worthing in *The Importance of Being Earnest*, a magnificently tormented Angelo in *Measure for Measure*, and a wonderfully wistful and foolish Gaev in *The Cherry Orchard*. Yet Gielgud, aristocrat that he was, knew how to let his

Courtesy of London Trust Productions

A television drama on the life of Wagner included a joint appearance by three great stage knights: Ralph Richardson (far left), Laurence Olivier (center), and John Gielgud. All great British actors prove themselves in the classics—as a young Olivier did in Hamlet *(far right) and as Derek Jacobi, a likely future knight, did in* Cyrano de Bergerac *(right) with the Royal Shakespeare Company.*

hair down on stage, as he did especially well as the incredibly seedy Spooner opposite Ralph Richardson's Hirst in *No Man's Land* by Harold Pinter.

Which leaves Olivier, who is nothing less than a grand theater pipe organ, capable of changing his voice, his looks, his style—capable of nothing less than quite literally pulling out all the stops. Consider the man's diverse stage achievements: a gleefully evil Richard III; a toweringly tragic

detractors would call it bravado), which is no less than one would expect from a true knight.

One yearns, of course, to speculate on theatrical knights yet-to-be. A prime candidate is Ian McKellen. He has assiduously tackled the toughest classical roles (including, within a few years of each other, a boyishly romantic Romeo and a deeply neurotic Macbeth), acted with both the National Theatre and the Royal Shakespeare Company, served as an actor-

the crafty, stuttering emperor in the BBC's mammoth series *I, Claudius.* Alan Howard, whose work has been confined largely to the British stage, qualifies as one of his generation's most spellbinding and heroic actors.

Still another strong candidate is Ben Kingsley, whose Academy Award for Best Actor in the title role of *Gandhi* cemented a reputation already well-established on the London stage. And the youthful daring of Antony Sher strongly suggests the huge

promise of his talent, following as he did his 1984 *Richard III* at the RSC (the most highly acclaimed performance of the role since Olivier's, forty years earlier) with a brave and brilliant portrayal of a New York drag queen in the British premiere of Harvey Fierstein's *Torch Song Trilogy.* Different as they are, this new crop of potential future knights of the British theater shares with stage knights of old an eternal quest for excellence in their intensely human art.

Donald Cooper/London

Oedipus, daringly performed on a double bill with the role of the inutterably foppish Mr. Puff in Sheridan's *The Critic*; a brooding, sinister Macbeth, considered by many to be the definitive performance of that role; the sleazy song-and-dance man Archie Rice in John Osborne's *The Entertainer.* No role has seemed to daunt Olivier, no theatrical challenge been a match for his bravery (some

manager at the National, prepared and toured his highly personal one-man tour de force *Acting Shakespeare* throughout the world, and made selective appearances in film and television. Derek Jacobi is another likely knight, valued both for his many fine romantic stage performances (including a superb Cyrano in 1983–84) as well as a body of TV work epitomized by his portrayal of

WIT IS THE COMMON CURRENCY of the British stage, and just as gold reserves support a nation's currency, so does Britain's theater heritage provide a solid-gold foundation for modern playwrights. Shakespeare's plays abound with puns and stunning turns of phrase. Playwrights of the Restoration period such as Richard Brinsley Sheridan (whose plays are still widely performed in Britain today) delighted in fine, clever conversation as much as in plot. In more recent years, the late Sir Noel Coward created an impressive body of work—from *Blithe Spirit* to *Private Lives* to *Design for Living*—that captured and epitomized the sophisticated repartée of the British upper class.

Today's crop of British playwrights have all the wit of their predecessors and more. With the demise of the Empire and Britain's evolution into a modern, socialist, socially-conscious society, its playwrights have become, in their own way, social crusaders, using wit to cut through the pretensions, snobberies, and injustices of the class system and contemporary life, while crafting plays with meaning as well as *bons mots.*

The changes were first rung in May of 1956, when John Osborne's *Look Back in Anger* debuted at the Royal Court Theatre in London. Its hero, Jimmy Porter, is a young man violently seeking to escape his working-class roots. The play's critical success heralded a new era of realism in British drama, and won its playwright—like his hero—the title of the first of the "angry young men."

David Storey literally raised realism to new heights with works like *The Contractor*, directed by filmmaker Lindsay Anderson in 1969 at the Royal Court. The story line involves the marriage of a contractor's daughter and its effects on the family; during the course of the play, a construction crew actually erects and tears down the canvas marquee beneath which the wedding takes place. Playwrights like Howard Brenton in *Weapons of Happiness* (staged at the National Theatre in 1976) and David Edgar with *Destiny* (the Royal Shakespeare Company at the Aldwych, then its London home, in 1977) painfully probe such starkly immediate topics as political repression and the rise of a new fascism in modern multi-racial Britain.

Issues and *ideas*, seriously explored, are revelled in by modern Brit-

Playwrights of Wit . . . and Conscience

The Raymond Mander & Joe Mitchenson Theatre Collection

ish playwrights. Harold Pinter, in modern classics like *The Birthday Party* (1958), *The Caretaker* (1960), *No Man's Land* (1975), and *Betrayal* (1978), presents some of the most penetrating yet enigmatic modern character studies ever written, their dialogue heavily laden with pauses that speak as eloquently as the author's words to express the psychological games we all play, and the insecurities we all harbor. David Hare's *Plenty* (1978) is a study of postwar disillusionment as seen through the eyes of a woman, from her days as a young secret agent in France during World War II to her success in the advertising world and the onslaught of near madness.

Women playwrights have also found their own resonant voices in modern Britain. Eighteen-year-old Shelagh Delaney caused a sensation with the 1958 London debut of her play *A Taste of Honey*—the story of a poor northern girl of seventeen, pregnant by a black sailor and comforted and cared for by a gay art student, while Pam Gems has become the most authoritative female voice in contemporary British theater. In works like *Piaf*—a 1978 biographical play with music of the life of the great French *chanteuse*—and her feminist reworking of Dumas's *fils' Camille* (1984), she has developed a style at once romantic and harshly realistic. Her plays both charm the audience and grab it by the throat.

Even in mainstream British comedy—a genre once typified by silly farcical romps involving frequently dropped trousers and an excess of sexual innuendo and double entendre—the British stage has found a new sophistication. This is

largely due to the works of Alan Ayckbourn, certainly the theater's greatest comic craftsman and breaker of new ground. In *The Norman Conquests* (1973–74), he examines the comic events of one weekend in a suburban home through not one but a trio of plays, each covering the same time span but in a different place—the dining room, the sitting room, and the garden. *Sisterly Feelings* (1980) has four different versions; the direction any one evening's performance takes is determined by a coin toss between two characters during the first act, and later by a spur-of-the-moment decision by the actor/character who won that toss. In such comically convoluted ways—and through the wry, unsentimental eye he casts on the foibles of the modern Briton—Ayckbourn continually adds depths of meaning to what was a shallow theatrical form.

Certainly the best-known and most widely respected of contemporary British playwrights is Tom Stoppard. His reputation came almost ready-made with his early play *Rosenkrantz and Guildenstern Are Dead* (which debuted in 1966 as a "fringe" production at Edinburgh's annual summer arts festival), a retelling of Shakespeare's *Hamlet* as seen through the eyes of two minor characters, the Danish prince's college chums. A witty, dramatically gripping work, it delights in intellectual wordplay and existential musings. In subsequent works, Stoppard has boldly tackled difficult topics, combined and presented with extravagantly daring wit and real theatrical craft. They include: *Jumpers* (a work about a futuristic British totalitarian state and a doddering old philosopher, with, not

incidentally, an amateur gymnastics team made up of philosophy professors); *Travesties* (which throws together Lenin, James Joyce, surrealist poet Tristan Tzara, and minor British Embassy offical Henry Carr in World War I Zurich); *Every Good Boy Deserves Favour* (a portrait of Communist oppression of the individual, performed with a full symphony

orchestra on stage and original music by André Previn); and *The Real Thing* (a play about a playwright writing plays about his own loves and marriages). In Stoppard's work, the verbal cleverness is undeniably, indelibly British; and, like many of his contemporaries, his wit forms a substantial framework for real, solid, modern content.

Donald Cooper/London

Noel Coward starred in 1939 with husband-and-wife team Alfred Lunt and Lynn Fontanne (left) in his play **Design for Living,** *a daring, witty look at an unconventionally well-adjusted love triangle.*

Tom Stoppard's play **The Real Thing,** *produced in 1984 with Roger Rees and Felicity Kendal in the leads (above), wrestled with the fundamental issues of true love and marital fidelity.*

Musicals: Before and After the Drought

FOR ALMOST A CENTURY, A GREAT musical drought afflicted the British stage. No significant stage musicals of world-class stature were produced —only gentle, inconsequential if charming works like *Me and My Girl*, *Mr. Cinders*, *The Boyfriend*, and *Oliver!* The hottest tickets on London's stages were invariably imports from Broadway. But flanking that gulf on either side are prodigious talents and remarkable undertakings that have made the British musical an innovator in the medium.

In 1875, the London theatrical impresario Richard D'Oyly Carte commissioned the successful dramatist W.S. Gilbert to write a cantata entitled *Trial by Jury*, the music for which was to be provided by the composer Arthur Sullivan, best known at the time for his sacred music. Thus was born the first successful Gilbert and Sullivan comic opera (the two men had collaborated six years earlier on a minor and unsuccessful work, *Thespis*). Over the course of the next two decades, during the golden years of Queen Victoria's reign, Gilbert and Sullivan would create—under the auspices of D'Oyly Carte—eleven

more musical classics, typified by Sullivan's bright, lilting melodies and Gilbert's witty lyrics, which seemed to have a music of their own. *H.M.S. Pinafore*, a "nautical comic opera," had an initial London run of almost two years, and the tale of a common sailor's love for the captain's daughter caused nothing short of "Pinafore mania" on Broadway. The same was true of *The Pirates of Penzance*, with its cast of amiable cutthroats led by the bumbling Pirate King, which premiered in Britain and New York on December 30 and 31, 1879, respectively. *Patience*, *Ruddigore*, *The Mikado*, *The Gondoliers*, *The Yeomen of the Guard*: all have become classics of the musical stage, and are still performed regularly in Britain and throughout the world.

Just as Gilbert and Sullivan's works dominated the stages of London and New York in the 1870s and 1880s, so a hundred years later have the works of one Briton—Andrew Lloyd Webber—completely annihilated all competition on the musical stage. Lloyd Webber began his writing career in the late 1960s with lyricist Tim Rice on *Joseph and the*

The Raymond Mander & Joe Mitchenson Theatre Collection

Weidenfeld Archives/The Theatre Museum

Appearing appropriately side-by-side on the witness stand in the caricature (far left), W.S. Gilbert (on the left) and Arthur Sullivan first collaborated on the cantata Trial by Jury. *Extravagant costumes and sets were common in the duo's stage works (near left). But, the modern stagecraft seen in such Andrew Lloyd Webber musicals as* Cats *(below) is even more exotic.*

Donald Cooper/London

Amazing Technicolor Dreamcoat, a light-hearted retelling of biblical tales in a musical pastiche that included country-western tunes, bright pop ditties, and even a hip-gyrating Pharaoh-Elvis. The partners' international reputations soared in 1970 with *Jesus Christ Superstar*, a full-fledged rock opera, and became fixed in the musical firmament for-ever with *Evita*, a worldwide hit based on the life of Argentinian dictator Juan Peron's second wife, Eva.

The two men split after that show, but Lloyd Webber went on to compose hit after megahit—including *Cats*, based on T.S. Eliot's whimsical poems about felines; *Starlight Express*, a show performed entirely on roller skates by a cast portraying an assortment of locomotives and railway cars in a lively retelling of the children's story *The Little Engine That Could*; and *Song and Dance*, about an English girl's life and loves in America. All of them display Lloyd Webber's uncanny ability to combine one of the English-speaking world's surest grasps of pop-songwriting with a solid, sophisticated classical sensibility and unparalleled showmanship that is admired world-wide.

With the advent of Andrew Lloyd Webber, the long drought in British musicals was over. And though an empire has dissolved during the century following Gilbert and Sullivan's fabled partnership, Britain is at least, once again, colonizing the world's stages with spectacular performance.

The Royal Ballet

IN OVER MORE THAN HALF A CENtury of growth and refinement, Britain's Royal Ballet has grown to become one of the greatest dance companies in the world. Just a handful of other national companies—among them the Leningrad Kirov and the New York City Ballet—are as large or as capable of mounting such classics of ballet theater as *Swan Lake, Sleeping Beauty, Coppelia, Giselle,* or *The Nutcracker* on a regular basis.

Such phenomenal abilities in a dance company usually come about in one of two ways. Some, like the American Ballet Theater, set out to gather together as many star dancers and choreographers as possible under one roof, to build a company with a broad base spanning past, present, and future talents. Others, typified by the New York City Ballet, pin their hopes on a single genius— in its case George Balanchine, whom Lincoln Kirstein imported from Russia to create a company in his own unique image.

With typical British ingenuity, the Royal Ballet forged a third path to greatness, a compromise of the other two. Dame Ninette de Valois founded what was then called the Sadler's Wells Ballet in 1931 with the deliberate intention of not only preserving past classics and offering pretty and inspiring entertainments, but also experimenting with and expanding the frontiers of balletic art. To give her fledgling company traditions where British dance had none worth speaking of, she hired Nicolai Serguff away

Royal Opera House/Debenham

from St. Petersburg's Maryinsky Theatre to establish a repertoire of classics at the Sadler's Wells Ballet. The company began to tour extensively, singlehandedly establishing the worldwide popularity of such full-length ballets as *Swan Lake* and *Sleeping Beauty*—introducing them to audiences in New York and Paris before the Bolshoi or Kirov Ballets had ever set toe outside of Russia.

Dame Ninette began to build on this classical foundation. In 1935, she picked Frederick Ashton as principal choreographer, adding modern, entirely British touches to the company's character. Such Ashton works as *Ondine, La Fille mal Gardee, The Dream, Daphnis and Chloe, Scenes de Ballet,* and *A Wedding Bouquet* helped create a British dance style. Sir Frederick became director of the

Royal Ballet in the early 1960s, continuing the pursuit of Dame Ninette's goals. Other noteworthy modern choreographers such as John Cranko and Kenneth MacMillan were also invited to create works to add to the Royal Ballet's contemporary collection of works.

But beyond its classic and contemporary repertoires, the Royal Ballet has been blessed with extraordi-

Camera Press, London

nary dancers—artists who have ultimately defined the company's greatness in the eyes of the public. The most illustrious partnership in the company's history was that of British-born Dame Margot Fonteyn and the Russian Rudolf Nureyev. Dame Margot's Juliet—a fragile, childlike, overwhelmingly touching performance that she continued to dance brilliantly well into middle age—found its perfect tragic counterpart in the athletic, heroic yet sensitive dancing of Nureyev's Romeo. When the two performed together, it was not uncommon for them to receive more than thirty curtain calls.

The Royal Ballet grows and changes even as it maintains its links with the past and with Dame Ninette's creative vision. New stars come and go. From the ranks of the company, Anthony Dowell assumed its directorship after being *premier danseur* for more than twenty years. On the firm foundation built by his predecessors, the Royal Ballet continues to be that wonderful paradox—a truly classical company on the cutting edge of artistic expression.

Douane *(left)* was one of the early Sadler's Wells Ballet productions staged in 1933 starring Dame Ninette de Valois and Robert Helpmann. In 1931, Dame Ninette founded the company, which was the forerunner to today's Royal Ballet, with the goal of bringing modern elements to balletic art.

Recent Royal Ballet stars have included Rudolf Nureyev and Margot Fonteyn, shown above in Romeo and Juliet, *and Anthony Dowell, whose leading roles have included* Afternoon of a Faun *(right).*

Zoë Dominic

benjamin BRITTEN

Nocturne

The Holy Sonnets of John Donne • A Birthday Hansel

PETER PEARS • BENJAMIN BRITTEN

London Symphony Orchestra

Chapter 7
Music

Folk Traditions

AT PRECISELY 5:50 A.M. EACH working day, early risers and insomniacs who tune into the BBC's news and magazine program, Radio Four, hear an admirable and wide-ranging five minutes of traditional national tunes. The selection never varies, the high point being "Greensleeves" and "What Shall We Do With the Drunken Sailor?" played simultaneously. This inspired blending virtually sums up the predominant qualities of British music—emotion and beauty, an emphasis on melody, and a leavening of good humor.

National music is, of course, a questionable concept. Dvorak's *New World Symphony*—its famous second movement in particular—is, after all, not really American. The composer, though inspired by America, labeled his work "genuine Bohemian music." Or is it just music?

Music was certainly not "just music" to the Elizabethans. They were "ravished" by it. Shakespeare's plays have many cues for music and actual songs. "It Was a Lover and His Lass" in *As You Like It* (Act V, scene iii) was set to music by Shakespeare's contemporary, Thomas Morley, a famous composer of madrigals—especially cheerful ones, a characteristically English quality. Wilbye, Byrd, Gibbons, Weelkes, and company made it a very tuneful age.

Nearly a century later, Henry Purcell surpassed them all. He composed the first—and the last for more than two hundred years—great native opera, *Dido and Aeneas*, whose lighter moments, especially a jolly sailor's song, are certainly representative of the English tradition.

After Purcell's death, only folk music survived (excluding the work of Handel, an adopted Englishman). Serious British composers were musical pygmies compared to the giants of European music. Happily, however, the second half of the nineteenth century saw the arrival of those very British products, the Savoy Operas of Gilbert and Sullivan, works as fine as Offenbach's operettas, though without the sex.

National Portrait Gallery, London

National Portrait Gallery, London

The best of British composers have never lost touch with their national roots. Henry Purcell (above) is memorialized in the name of the small recital hall in London's South Bank arts complex, The Purcell Room. The music of Ralph Vaughan Williams (left) is interwoven with traditional folk melodies. Benjamin Britten (right) wrote contemporary arrangements of many old British folk songs and composed major orchestral and operatic works as well.

Salvation was at hand for a revived British music scene. British composers went back to their roots, the roots of folk melody, and Parry, Stanford, Mackenzie, and Elgar forced themselves on the attention of the British musical public in the closing years of the nineteenth century.

Sir Edward Elgar stood above all others. His *Enigma Variations*, *The Dream of Gerontius*, *Falstaff*, two symphonies, violin and cello concertos, as well as his lighter music, all became hugely popular and remain greatly loved. The *Enigma Variations* —musical portraits of Elgar's friends—*feel* English; indeed, the "Nimrod Variation" is a national glory, as is his march "Land of Hope and Glory," though the jingoistic words (*not* Elgar's doing) are nowadays frowned upon in some quarters.

Germany was the first foreign nation to hail Elgar's genius, his *First Symphony* being in the European tradition. Yet *Falstaff* is Shakespeare's rotund English anti-hero brought to life, and Elgar's oratorio *The Dream of Gerontius* sounds happiest when heard in an English cathedral. Many devotees of Elgar's work claim to "see" the composer's beloved Malvern Hills in several of his pieces.

The links to folk music are unarguable in the work of Ralph Vaughan Williams, born in 1872, fifteen years after Elgar. His *London Symphony*, first heard in 1914, is just that—a musical portrait of the city and its sounds, all fully annotated by the composer. His *Fantasia on a Theme of Thomas Tallis*, premiered in Gloucester Cathedral, uses a noble Tudor tune and is, indeed, a veritable cathedral in sound. Vaughan Williams's growing international reputation can be seen in the fact that André Previn has recorded all nine of his symphonies.

In the first half of this century, Sir William Walton marked a return to the European mainstream. Yet he also remained distinctively British. The *Portsmouth Point* overture is as bracing as a seaside walk, while *Façade* is marvelously inventive—a Lancashire lad having sophisticated fun. Walton's *Belshazzar's Feast* is in the great tradition of British chorale and, more than half a century after it was written, remains electrifying.

Britain's two great postwar composers are Sir Michael Tippett and the late Benjamin Britten. Of the two, folk music meant far more to Britten, a most English composer. The North Sea suffuses *Peter Grimes* and sea shanties are heard in *Billy Budd*. Shakespeare's Warwickshire can be found in the opera *A Midsummer Night's Dream*. Britten and Peter Pears continually performed the composer's arrangements of traditional folk songs, and though he is gone, through his music Benjamin Britten remains a national treasure.

benjamin BRITTEN

LONDON ENTERPRISE

Nocturne
The Holy Sonnets of John Donne ⋅ A Birthday Hansel
PETER PEARS ⋅ BENJAMIN BRITTEN
London Symphony Orchestra

Decca International

A Selected Discography

Those wishing to explore the delights of British classical music would do well to begin with the following recordings:

Edward Elgar. *Cello Concerto* and *Enigma Variations*. Daniel Barenboim conducting the Philadelphia Orchestra; Jacqueline du Pre, soloist. (CBS 76529).

Ralph Vaughan Williams. *A London Symphony*. André Previn conducting the London Symphony Orchestra. (GL 89690).

William Walton. *Belshazzar's Feast*. Sir George Solti conducting the London Philharmonic Orchestra and Choir; Benjamin Luxon, soloist. (SET 618).

Benjamin Britten. *Peter Grimes*. Sir Colin Davis conducting the Chorus and Orchestra of the Royal Opera House, Covent Garden; Jon Vicker in the title role. (SXL 2150).

BRITAIN WAS NEVER THE "LAND without music" that some German musicians claimed it was in the early nineteenth century. The slur was probably due to the lack of opera houses at a time when the amateur choral society, complete with its annual Christmas performance of Handel's *Messiah*, was a British specialty. Such choral societies still exist in

House, Covent Garden, is shared by the Royal Opera and the Royal Ballet. Its greatest nights are as spectacular as any in the operatic world. Joan Sutherland rocketed to fame there as Lucia di Lammermoor in 1959. The spirits of Caruso, Melba, and Callas are still felt there. Less star-studded but more operatically theatrical on a regular basis is the English National

Opera at the Coliseum in London, its most famous production reckoned to be Dr. Jonathon Miller's Mafia-style *Rigoletto*. Excellent opera is also staged by the Scottish Opera, Opera North, and, especially, the Welsh National Opera. The world-famous Glyndebourne Festival of opera, held each summer since 1934 on the grounds of a private estate in Sussex,

is next to impossible to get into, but televised performances console the masses, at least somewhat. And after the season ends, younger Glynde-bourne singers assume the leading roles and take the operas on tour throughout Britain.

How British are British performers? Although they do not have as great a national repertoire as

Great Performers and Performances

Britain, the most renowned being the incomparable Huddersfield Choral Society, adored by professional musicians, which celebrated its centennial in 1986.

Today London is home to four major orchestras: the Philharmonia; the London Symphony; the London Philharmonic, founded by the great Sir Thomas Beecham; and the Royal Philharmonic, which was the last orchestra formed by Beecham. The BBC has a number of orchestras, most notably the BBC Symphony, the London Baroque Ensemble, the London Sinfonietta, and the Academy of St.-Martin-in-the-Fields. The most famous orchestras outside London are the Hallé in Manchester, founded in 1857; the Scottish National Orchestra; and the City of Birmingham Symphony, whose brilliant young conductor, Simon Rattle, had already achieved fame while in his teens.

London's historic Royal Opera

Godfrey MacDominic

The Photosource

The exuberant Simon Rattle (opposite) is one of a new generation of British conductors, while the great soprano Joan Sutherland rocketed to diva status with her 1959 Covent Garden appearance as Lucia di Lammermoor (left). The joy Britons take in music is seen most boldly at the Last Night of the Proms (below).

Godfrey MacDominic

some, they tend to be wide-ranging and versatile. There is no denying their quality, from younger players like the pianist Dennis Lill to veterans like Ida Haendel, one of a number of British artists born in Europe. And it is notably English to find the highest standards of performance among amateurs in a small Suffolk town, just as Welsh choirs have a fervor unmatched by the world's great professional ensembles.

But more British than the performers themselves are, perhaps, the events in which they perform. Most British of all are "the Proms," the Promenade Concerts founded by Sir Henry Wood (and approaching their one hundredth season in 1994) that are held in the huge Royal Albert Hall south of London's Kensington Gardens. It is an international series of concerts, running from mid-July to mid-September, with a colossal an-

nual repertoire and list of soloists from home and abroad. Standards are high, and the response from the "Promenaders," who stand in the vast seatless arena (or sit if there is room), is often wildly enthusiastic.

The Last Night of the Proms is a national institution. Promenaders sport funny hats and wave balloons, streamers, and Union Jacks. In spite of their antic attire, they give total concentration to the music during the first half of the concert. But after the intermission the audience goes wild. They sing, hum, and play along as the orchestra performs the founder's *Fantasia on British Sea Songs*; likewise for Elgar's *Land of Hope and Glory* and Parry's *Jerusalem*. It is one of the great British party nights, a musical extravaganza watched by millions at home and abroad on TV. British stiff upper lips, an exaggerated trait, are nowhere to be seen.

"Four Lads That Shook the World"

Camera Press, London

JUST A FEW BLOCKS AWAY FROM Liverpool's grim docklands, where ferries still crisscross the Mersey, a short walk through the dark and winding streets off Lime Street brings you to Mathew Street. There, in an alcove, stands a barely recognizable statue of Liverpool's most famous sons, looking to the heavens; beneath them, a plaque reads: FOUR LADS THAT SHOOK THE WORLD. In present-day Britain, Liverpool may increasingly be synonymous with urban turmoil, Tory victimization, and soccer fanaticism; but to the rest of the world, the city on the Mersey will always be the home of the Beatles. And for once the hyperbole can't be overdone. They really did change the world forever.

Enough has been written about John Lennon, Paul McCartney, George Harrison, and Ringo Starr (né Richard Starkey) to fill a small library. Music fans throughout the world know the story of how four lads from Liverpool's leafy suburbs fulfilled the hopes and dreams of their manager, Brian Epstein, to become "bigger than Elvis." But what people often forget is that, as international a phenomenon as they became, the Beatles could only have been British.

Britain in the 1950s was stultifyingly claustrophobic. American rebels like Elvis Presley, James Dean, Marlon Brando, and Chuck Berry had the wide open spaces of America in which to lose or transform themselves. English kids had the High Street, pubs, and coffeehouses. So they listened to American records, watched American movies and danced in the aisles, and formed bands as a way of getting out.

Bear in mind that this was a middle-class condition. Contrary to popular myth, the Beatles—particularly John Lennon—were not poor. A look at the handsome home in which Lennon was raised by his Auntie Mimi puts any question of poverty to rest. (Ringo is the only one of the four with any claim to being lower middle class.) And, as critic Simon Frith has pointed out, music in Britain is a cause for the middle classes; for the lower classes, it's simply a part of everyday life. So middle-class kids like the Beatles—not to mention the equally middle-class Rolling Stones—took up music with a vengeance.

Rock music of the 1950s and early 1960s was purely American, a combination and evolution of blues, country, gospel, and something more (perhaps the American spirit?). The British, as it was believed on both sides of the Atlantic, knew nothing. So, thousands of miles from the source, the Beatles copied the American music they loved—a little Elvis here, some Buddy Holly there, throw in a bit of Chuck Berry, Little Richard, and the Everly Brothers. But, from

John, Paul, George, and Ringo have the bright smiles of newborn success in this early photograph of them (far left).

As the 1960s grew more tumultuous, the Beatles reflected that change (below). John Lennon (left) was by far the most intellectually provocative and politically active Beatle. His successful solo career and happily reconciled life with Yoko Ono was cut short by Mark David Chapman in 1980.

the start, they added some distinctive guitar playing, a charming lilt that came to be known as the Mersey beat, and the indefinable genius that Lennon and McCartney catalyzed in each other. Soon, unexpectedly, they had created a sound and a look that became the yardstick by which other popular artists and music were measured. The famous Liverpool wit and unaffectedness made everyone else look stiff and stodgy by comparison. The Beatles were talented, creative, funny, and intelligent. If you weren't, you just didn't fit in.

Once they became confident enough of their own talent and ability to transcend their American influences, John and Paul began to explore themselves and their own country. "Penny Lane" and "Strawberry Fields" are literal evocations of the landscape of their boyhood memories. There really *is* a shelter in the

middle of the roundabout in Penny Lane, and Strawberry Fields *is* a dreamy, mysterious place.

Writing at last about their own experiences, the Beatles made Britain come alive for foreigners, evoking its richness and vitality. Young people saw an exciting, complex, modern culture where once they had seen only well-mannered restraint. With each successive record, the Beatles introduced the world to little-known bits of Brittania: Blackburn, Lancashire; the Albert Hall; the motor trade; the vaudeville tradition; Isle of Wight retirement homes; and, most obviously, Abbey Road.

For a long time, the Liverpool city fathers chose to ignore the luster and appeal the Beatles had given their city. Perhaps John Lennon's death in 1980 changed the civic mind. Now Liverpool has hundreds of Beatle-inspired attractions: statues, tours, exhibits, souvenir shops, and any other form of commercial exploitation that happens to be kicking around. Commerce aside, however, the city's pride in its "lads" is sincere and all-pervasive. Housewives regale visitors over lunch with tales of the Cavern Club, where the Beatles first performed, and pub denizens recall the group's high jinks and lean times with affectionate gusto.

The Beatles have been broken up now for more years than they were together. John Lennon is dead. Paul McCartney hides himself away in the countryside. George Harrison and Ringo Starr have settled into the obscurity of millionaire celebrities. But their songs, their recordings, and their personal legends remain as vivid as ever, permanently embellishing Britain's glory.

Camera Press, London

IT SEEMS THAT SINCE THE breakup of the Beatles, British pop music has spawned few, if any, legends. Sure, there has been great music from artists of note—Elvis Costello, the Pretenders, the Beat, Culture Club, Blue Nile, the Police (and their leader-gone-solo, Sting), Frankie Goes to Hollywood, Paul Young, Sade. There have been newsmaking pseudo-trendsetters like the late-1970s Sex Pistols and Johnny Rotten, patron devil of the short-lived Punk Rock movement. There have even been great gentlemen of rock: Bob Geldof, K.B.E. (an Irishman living and working in London, he was honored by the Queen as a Knight Commander of the British Empire in June of 1986) is a national hero for his visionary and selfless work to help the starving in Africa, and Billy Bragg and Paul Weller have been tireless in their support of the Labour Party and unemployed youth.

But the real trend of late in British

Visual Music

Garvin/Ron Galella Ltd. © 1985

pop has been *visual* music—the fast cuts, erratic narratives, incessant symbolism, and omnipresent musical background of pop videos. And it's not surprising that the most accomplished and well-known video directors in the world today—Godley and Creme, Steve Barron, David Mallet, and Tim Pope—are all British. The seeds of the phenomenon were sown in the 1960s by ex-adman Richard Lester's Beatle feature films, by the swinging advertising style of British commercials from that period, and by the British tradition of innovative and daring television. *A Hard Day's Night*, *Help!*, and virtually everything done by the Monty Python comedy troupe look positively prophetic to anyone who's seen a rock video.

Visual music is not, of course, a strictly British invention. It has been around, at least in concept, as long as there has been recorded sound; the use of visuals to advertise music began in Germany in the 1930s. But the rock promo film or video made with the express intention of promoting a record came to prominence in the U.K. and has been raised to new heights (or, depending on your outlook, lowered to new depths) by British directors and musical artists.

Common knowledge has it that the first record whose sales were appreciably affected by a video was Queen's "Bohemian Rhapsody," whose visual promo was directed by Bruce Gowers in 1975. The so-called special effects—split and resplit screens, heads appearing to drift off into infinity—look laughable now to sophisticated video junkies, but after the video was shown on the BBC's "Top of the Pops," the record soared to number one and stayed there for nine weeks. The incredible success of "Bo Rhap" led other bands to insist that their record companies provide them with videos, which cut the need for touring, didn't take too long to make, and more often than not presented bands in a flattering and exotic light.

The next milestone came in 1979. "I Don't Like Mondays" from The Boomtown Rats and featuring a choirboyish Bob Geldof, is cited by many of today's star video directors as the one that opened their imaginations to the possibilities video could afford. Stark and eerie, "Mondays" was the first video to feature a narrative, however skeletal, and present the band as actors and characters in their own musical creation.

Then came the avalanche. The New Romantic movement, risen from

the ashes of the self-prescribed death of Punk, was a natural for video. All puffed up with the concept of glamour and visual excess as ends in themselves, New Romantics were perfect fodder for directors like Australian expatriate Russell Mulchay, whose creation of the "Vienna" video for UltraVox ensured that smoke machine manufacturers, dry ice companies, and owners of crumbling castles would be rolling in money as long as there were record companies willing to foot the bill for such mini-epics. Mulchay was also the man responsible for the Duran Duran trilogy of "Rio," "Hungry Like a Wolf," and "Say a Prayer," described by Sex Pistols mastermind Malcolm McLaren as "designer manniquins walking the streets of Sri Lanka."

Such elaborate travelogues did more than merely make international superstars and pinup faves out of the Duran boys. They also established a whole new currency for rock performers, one not seen since the 1950s. Bands had to be good-looking, glamorous, and able to act if they were going to come across successfully in videos. Especially after the birth of MTV in the States, looking good in videos was crucial to a band's success. Thanks to British superiority in video-making and image presentation, homegrown bands like the Eurythmics, Culture Club, the Fixx, Human League, and Flock of Seagulls had million-selling hits.

British video directors became stars in their own right, and it wasn't long before they were called on to make videos for American artists. Steve Barron, director of the Truffaut inspired "Don't You Want Me" for Human League, was asked by Michael Jackson to direct "Billie Jean." The eccentric Tim Pope did the honors for the equally weird Neil Young. And Godley and Creme, arguably the biggest stars in the vid-director firmament, made an amazingly clever video using automatons for Herbie Hancock's "RockIt," transforming a respected but not-very-well-known jazz artist into a Top Ten star.

By the mid-1980s, videos had already peaked in terms of their impact on sales and style. Many groups defiantly decided to forego them and had hits regardless. But when early 1980s popular culture is reassessed, as it inevitably will be at some future date by thoughtful pundits, the brash, kinetic, frantic images that accompanied most of the popular music of the day will probably be seen as emblematic of an age.

Bob Geldof (far left), lead of rock video pioneers The Boomtown Rats, gained worldwide fame with his efforts to feed African drought victims through organizing the Live Aid concert in 1985.

Innovative videos promote songs by pop pinups like Duran Duran (center) and Eurythmics, the technopop duo whose vocalist, Annie Lennox (below), always delivers an electrifying and mesmerizing performance.

RCA/Columbia Pictures Video U.K.

Chapter 8
The Large and Small Screen

CYNICS MIGHT SAY THAT BRITAIN'S main role in early cinema history was to supply Hollywood with a steady stream of stars and supporting players. Chaplin, Colman, Donat, Grant, Garson, Milland, Niven, and, after the war, Mason, Granger, Simmons, Kerr, and Caine are just a handful of the stars. Any movie buff who requires the first names in this galaxy needs

Thirty-Nine Steps; and Anthony Asquith, a former prime minister's son who made such fine films as *Pygmalion*, starring Leslie Howard as Higgins, and the wartime classic *The Way to the Stars*.

In the doldrums of the 1930s, the British film industry was saved by a Hungarian, Alexander Korda; one might even say there was no British

film industry until Korda and his brothers, Zoltán and Vincent, moved in. They proceeded to challenge Hollywood itself. Korda was a producer of genius, creating some thirty films, including *The Ghost Goes West*, *The Scarlet Pimpernel*, *Things to Come*, *The Third Man*, *Richard III*, and *Hobson's Choice*, as well as directing *The Private Lives of Henry VIII* and *Rem-*

brandt. Korda, significantly, got his films shown in America. And, thanks to his friend Winston Churchill, who especially loved "Lady Hamilton" (*That Hamilton Woman*), he became Sir Alexander.

The cinema boomed in Britain during World War II, with war stories like Noel Coward's *In Which We Serve*, inspired by the exploits of Lord

A Cinematic Legacy

his credentials examined and a quick review of great movie actors.

Other cynics may recall that when the British cinema was booming in the 1940s and 1950s, as never before or since, most of the films made in Britain were never properly distributed in America outside its major cities. It was alleged the folks in the Midwest would never understand them, though with Limeys as thick on the ground as ever in Hollywood, this was either gross ignorance or discrimination. Yet, ironically, it was the rude, lewd *Carry On* film comedies, with their broad gags and regional accents, that helped break down the cultural barriers and inspire an appreciation of British cinema.

The British film industry was founded in the 1890s, its biggest early hit being *Rescued by Rover* (1905), a title that pretty much explains itself. Two major talents emerged from the silent era in Britain: Alfred Hitchcock, who settled in Hollywood in 1940 but never lost his British roots, accent, or sly humor, and whose strictly British legacy includes *The Lady Vanishes* and *The*

Still from *Brief Encounter*, Courtesy of the Rank Organization PLC

In **Brief Encounter** *(left), directed by David Lean, Celia Johnson and Trevor Howard find romance in a railway station. Comedy is the dominant note in Robert Hamer's* **Kind Hearts and Coronets,** *one of the greatest of the Ealing comedies, starring Alec Guinness (right).*

Mountbatten, and *The Way Ahead,* which starred David Niven. New stars emerged: James Mason and Stewart Granger, who would go to California, Margaret Lockwood and Phyllis Calvert, who did not. Most British of all was Celia Johnson, who starred with Trevor Howard in that understated classic *Brief Encounter,* directed by David Lean. Soon thereafter, Carol Reed gained fame for directing *Odd Man Out* and *The Fallen Idol.*

Most British films at that time were notable for their restraint. But the Ealing comedies came along to demonstrate another aspect of the British character—the wry humor that seems to come naturally from a people so caught up in appearances. The prim Michael Balcon was their very creative producer. He had a brilliant group of directors, most notably American-born Alexander Mackendrick, a writer-director responsible for *Whiskey Galore, The Man in the White Suit,* and *The Ladykillers.* Robert Hamer directed the great *Kind Hearts and Coronets,* with Alec Guinness playing an entire family of eccentric characters.

Cannon Street Entertainment Ltd.

©1967 Metro-Goldwyn-Mayer Inc.

Courtesy of Columbia Pictures Corporation Ltd.

Julie Christie and Alan Bates (above) enchanted audiences in John Schlesinger's screen adaptation of the Thomas Hardy novel Far From the Madding Crowd. Gandhi *(right), directed by Sir Richard Attenborough and starring Ben Kingsley, swept the Academy Awards for 1982, including Best Screenplay, Best Picture, Best Director, and Best Actor.*

Neil Jordan's 1986 film Mona Lisa *came from nowhere to win Cockney star Bob Hoskins (opposite page, left) Best Actor at Cannes and an Academy Award nomination.* My Beautiful Laundrette *(opposite page, right), starring Daniel Day Lewis (at left) and Saeed Jaffrey, garnered acclaim for its portrayal of the tensions that can arise in a relationship between a working-class white and an Indian immigrant in suburban London.*

Despite crises, the British film industry has survived admirably. In the 1960s, the James Bond series brought new attention to Britain; the early movies, such as *Dr. No* and *Goldfinger*, had a distinctively understated British flavor, nothing like the international romps that followed.

The new wave of realism in British theater that followed John Osborne's *Look Back in Anger* in 1956 was reflected in the cinema, including a film of that play, starring Richard Burton. David Lean added to the new quality image of British cinema with *The Bridge on the River Kwai*, starring Alec Guinness, and *Lawrence of Arabia*, which made a star of Peter O'Toole. New names emerged to challenge the best of the world's directors: John Schlesinger, for example, with *Far From the Madding Crowd* and Joseph Losey with *The Go-Between*.

In recent years young directors like David Puttnam have kept the legacy alive with *Chariots of Fire*, which won the Academy Award for Best Picture (1981), as did veteran director Sir Richard Attenborough's *Gandhi* the following year. Still other directors are making films that reflect social and political changes in modern Britain. For example, Stephen Frears's *My Beautiful Laundrette*, originally shot for television, became a critical and commercial success in first-run cinemas with its story of racial tensions and working-class strife in suburban London. Neil Jordan's *Mona Lisa*, a bittersweet gangster drama set in the demimonde of London, won its star, stocky Cockney Bob Hoskins, world-wide accolades. None of the old concerns about people being able to understand a distinctively British product seem to matter anymore. What does matter is quality filmmaking, for which the British still seem to have a talent. The inheritors of Britain's cinematic legacy are doing their predecessors proud.

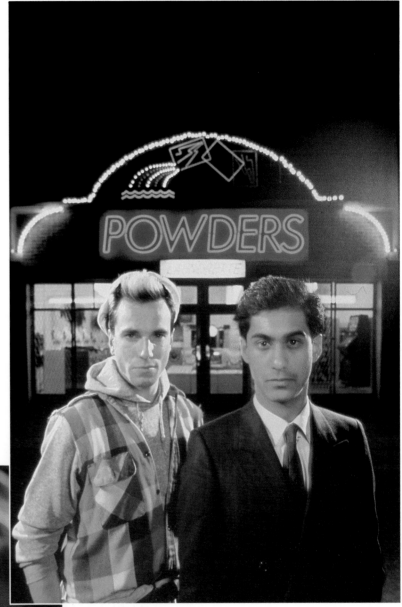

Channel Four Television

Courtesy of Handmade Films

Televised Masterpieces

London Weekend Television

BRITISH TELEVISION AUDIENCES are offered a spectacular range of programs on which to feast their eyes and, not infrequently, their minds. Given the immense expertise and talents of Britain's television industry—a complex affair that basically comprises BBC Television and its rivals, the commercial ITV (Independent Television) network and Channel Four Television—many Britons are prone to regard their small screen fare as "the least worst in the world." Chauvinism aside, what is undeniable is that at its best British television produces masterly works. When lapped by the more forgettable trivia that can invade viewing hours, those masterpieces stand out boldly.

Foremost among the serial dramas that have been popular and critical successes are "Upstairs, Downstairs," a saga of life in an upper-class household from Edwardian times to the 1920s; "Brideshead Revisited," a dramatization of Evelyn Waugh's 1945 novel by ITV; and "The Jewel in the Crown." The latter, based on a four-novel epic, *The Raj Quartet* by Paul Scott, was set in India in the last years before its independence. Screened in fourteen one-hour episodes, "The Jewel in the Crown" brought Scott's work vividly to life with its gallery of memorable characters played by the cream of

British and Indian acting talent. As with a number of domestic productions, its essentially British qualities lie in its literary origins, faithfulness to the original text, and subtle exploration of class distinctions. The issue of imperialism gave "Jewel" an extra, tragic dimension that elevated it to the rank of a true classic.

Actors, producers, and designers

Granada Television

Channel Four Television

The best of British television drama miraculously portrays the extraordinary side of everyday life. "Upstairs, Downstairs" (above left) gave equal time to both the servants' quarters and the master's domain of an upper-class household. "The Jewel in the Crown" (left) chronicled the human side of the Empire's end in India. In "The Naked Civil Servant" (above), John Hurt portrayed the homosexual Quentin Crisp's one-man sexual revolution.

range from "The Six Wives of Henry VIII" and "Elizabeth R" to the personal and public dramas of "Edward VII" and "Edward and Mrs. Simpson," impeccably stylish accounts of two twentieth-century royals.

In the world of documentaries, it was Britain that evolved the blockbuster variety in which a single person expounded on a favorite topic. Sir Kenneth Clark ("Civilization"), Jacob Bronowski ("The Ascent of Man"), and David Attenborough ("Life on Earth" and "The Living Planet") all handled vast canvases with warmth, urbanity, and deep knowledge, not to say miles of superb footage. ITV's mighty "World at War" was voiced-over by England's most distinguished actor, Sir Laurence Olivier. More recently, the genesis of modern art was charted in "The Shock of the New"; Iberian conflict in "The Spanish Civil War"; and the cultural history of the dark continent in a series about Africa. Such productions have made a giant imprint on television culture, and giant inroads into mass education.

Yet, ultimate laurels should perhaps go to those more modest offerings that have touched the heart as well as the intellect: the endearing, poetry-quoting barrister, "Rumpole of the Bailey" (based on the novels of barrister-playwright John Mortimer); "The Naked Civil Servant," which sensitively followed the early life of the flamboyant homosexual Quentin Crisp, brilliantly portrayed by John Hurt; and "Pennies from Heaven," Dennis Potter's bittersweet six-part account of a sheet-music salesman, played by Bob Hoskins, with a 1930s song in his heart and a lustful twinkle in his eye.

often bring to television the experience gained by working in the theater, as evidenced by an eye for sets and costume detail as well as the power of performances both bravura and understatement. It is the characteristic English penchant for understatement that adds such resonance to quality British productions. As for subject matter, the whole of British literature and history is there to be tapped. Royalty has proved a winning theme. Elaborate costume dramas

Televised Mayhem

WHEN "MONTY PYTHON'S FLYING Circus" burst upon the small screen in homes all over Britain in 1969, a legend in modern British television comedy was born. Its members— John Cleese, Graham Chapman, Eric Idle, Terry Jones, Michael Palin, and animator Terry Gilliam—combined to create the most anarchic and zany series ever seen on the British screen. Sketches such as Cleese's Ministry of Silly Walks and the encounter between a pet-shop owner and an irate customer protesting that he has been sold a dead parrot

("This is an *ex*-parrot!") were representative of the kind of hilarious absurdity that won the show cult status around the world. Its opening catch-phrase, "And now for Something Completely Different," meant just that. The Pythons' surrealism, silliness, and love of outrageous parody revealed a strain in the richly idiosyncratic nature of British humor that went back to Britain's music-hall days, to the nonsense verse of Edward Lear and the satirical lyrics of W.S. Gilbert.

A more concrete and revolutionary

REB 260 (LP)/RMC 4055 (MC) © BBC 1976

REB/REMC 73 BBC CD 73 © BBC 1970

With John Cleese, Michael Palin, Grahame Chapman, Eric Idle, Terry Jones, Carol Cleveland *from the BBC Television Series*

influence was the 1950s BBC radio series "The Goon Show," whose sheer aural lunacy, whipped up by eccentric geniuses Peter Sellers, Spike Milligan, and Harry Secombe, made converts even of the Royal Family (Prince Charles is notorious for his Goon impressions). After the Python series, manic humor again surfaced memorably in "Fawlty Towers," in which John Cleese played Basil Fawlty, proprietor of a small Devonshire hotel. A walking disaster area, Fawlty was by turns servile, tyrannical, and hysterical, a pent-up cy-

clone of neuroses forever misunderstood by his hapless Spanish waiter, Manuel, and barely tolerated by his wife, Sybil. For many, Fawlty was one of television's most grotesque comic creations, a distillation of the many characters Cleese developed with the Python gang.

The spirit of irreverence that so marked "Monty Python" flourishes in a diverse collection of British television performers: in the lecherous romps of Benny Hill, the camp clowning of Kenny Everett, and the archly risqué humor of Frankie Howerd. By

Record sleeves reproduced by permission of BBC Enterprises Ltd., London

"Monty Python's Flying Circus" (far left), Britain's surrealistic comedy show of the 1970s, was inspired by 1950s comedians Peter Sellers, Spike Milligan, and Harry Secombe who starred in BBC radio's "The Goon Show" (below right). Another zany 1950s performer was Tony Hancock (left) who was, until his suicide in 1968, Britain's favorite comedian. Another brand of British humor, caricature reaches its zenith in "Spitting Image," with biting satire of public figures like Prime Minister Margaret Thatcher (below left).

contrast, the situation comedies of 1950s' comic Tony Hancock (who committed suicide in 1968), occupy a different niche in British humor. Hancock's on-screen persona of the lugubrious loner filled with false bravado and delusions of grandeur made him Britain's most lovable funny man.

In the 1980s, three shows in particular attained great popularity. "Not the Nine O'Clock News," winner of the Silver Rose at Montreux in 1980 for the most innovative program, produced sharp skits heavily laced with rudeness and fashionable cynicism. Conventional sitcom veered into the realm of the neo-psychotic with "The Young Ones," in which four friends—among them a wild caricature of an English punk and a glum-faced no-hoper—share a house with chaotic

results. It was a style of humor developed by Britain's new-wave "alternative" comedians like Rik Mayall.

For ferocious satire, however, nothing equals the weekly television revue "Spitting Image." Its cast of four hundred or so latex-and-foam-rubber puppets, created by master-caricaturists Peter Fluck and Roger Law, send up every topical event and famous name with unsparing vitriol. Prime Minister Margaret Thatcher, wearing a business suit and smoking a Churchillian cigar, is shown as a tough taskmistress dominating a cabinet of squabbling ministerial toadies, while President Reagan is forever hunting for his missing brain or blowing up the world. In this land of fervent monarchists, even the denizens of Buckingham Palace come in for their share of lampooning.

© Central Independent Television plc. 1984

REB/REMC 142 © BBC 1972.

The BBC presents
THE LAST GOON SHOW OF ALL

BBC records STEREO

Chapter 9
Arts and Crafts

Rural and Romantic Traditions

IN A WORLD THAT IS EVER MORE complicated, cynical, and claustrophobically urban, the great art of Britain's past speaks to us vividly, with a message of simplicity, nostalgia, and a love for the open spaces of the countryside. Many British artists and poets in the eighteenth and nineteenth centuries idealized man's relationship to nature, a direct response to the threat posed by the Industrial Revolution. Civilization, they felt, was mankind's fall.

The notion of pastoral bliss comes across clearly in the works of the nineteenth-century painter Samuel Palmer. Peasants contentedly glean the corn, or village folk return home from church across the ripening fields as an early moon rises in the dusky sky. Palmer's simple, direct paintings expressed well the thoughts of his teacher, the visionary poet and painter William Blake, who called for imagination to oppose the deadening forces of modern "reason." Blake, in both his poems and his paintings (sometimes combined, as in his *Songs of Innocence and Experience*), abhorred the "dark Satanic Mills" of modern industry, and dreamed of building a new Jerusalem "In England's green and pleasant land."

The poet William Wordsworth greatly developed the cult of nature in the nineteenth century, celebrating in-stinct over reason and describing the beauties of his Lake District home in simple, direct fashion. And no closer parallel could be found to Wordsworth's poems than the paintings of his contemporary John Constable. The son of a miller, Constable immersed himself in the countryside of his native Suffolk, painting lush scenes of woods and streams, horses and carts. His genius lay in a specific quality of light he achieved through intense observation; when the light changed on a scene he was painting, he would only continue with that canvas when the desired lighting returned. Constable's paintings—particularly *The Hay Wain* in the National Gallery—may well be the closest many of us will ever come to understanding the true experience of a rural way of life in Britain.

While Constable's contemporary J.M.W. Turner also depicted a rural England, Turner's real predilection seems to have been more for the romantic extremes of dramatic landscapes (much as the poet Lord Byron used mountainous scenery for dramatic effect). Turner's revolutionary later work almost loses itself in the watery incandescence of setting suns and the multicolored frenzy of stormy seas—a self-assured wildness of technique that many of Turner's detractors chose to read as a sign of

Tate Gallery

Tate Gallery

Nineteenth-century British artists captured the romance of their nation's countryside. Samuel Palmer evoked a sense of mystery and silence in Coming from Evening Church *(left).* John Constable's Hampstead Heath with a Rainbow *(right) portrayed the splendor of storm and sunlight.* J.M.W. Turner's Yacht Approaching the Coast *(below) typifies the artist's bold, impressionistic view.*

Tate Gallery

madness in the artist. Turner's colors and brushstrokes are indeed wild, executed with such spectacularly intense passion that they managed to fuse the rural with the romantic, throwing off an energy that remains undiminished today.

It may seem a curious step from Turner to the Pre-Raphaelite Brotherhood, which was creating its own artistic revolution even as Turner lay dying. Dissimilar though their styles were, they had in common a continuing interest in the English countryside. But while Turner's landscapes mirrored his spirit, the Pre-Raphaelites used rural landscapes as a setting for moralistic tales. These artists—particularly Millais, Rossetti, and Holman-Hunt—attempted to make art, as it had been in times past, once again a conveyor of moral principle. They used romantic themes to instill a sense of pathos in the viewer: Who could not be moved, for example, by Millais's painting of Ophelia (from Shakespeare's *Hamlet*) floating downstream to her death, garlanded with wildflowers?

The Pre-Raphaelites' paintings were a curious mixture of medieval-style pageantry, Christian doctrine, and Victorian respectability, and always relied upon the viewer's grasp of a surface storyline and its deeper meanings. In Pre-Raphaelite works, you can always rely upon sheep to signify the human race in need of shepherding from God, a field of poppies to represent death, and so on. Aided, perhaps, by a little prompting on the particulars of such rural symbolism, a modern museumgoer can still grasp the point of Pre-Raphaelite art while wholly enjoying the virtuosity of its technique.

Contemporary Artists

MORE THAN A CENTURY AFTER the heyday of romanticism and ruralism, it seems that the pendulum in British art has swung again toward a closer connection with life and humanity—albeit with a thoroughly modern give-and-take between reality and imagination.

David Hockney lucidly portrays realistic subjects with a joyously vivid palette that seems to reflect the influence of his present home high in the hills above Hollywood and Beverly Hills. His pictures display a simple, happy, straightforward intimacy with his subject matter—be it friends, hotel rooms, or his trademark swimming pools. He offers a sun-filled world where hedonistic distraction denies a foothold to despair.

Hockney has shown his inventiveness and his spectacular technical mastery through the great variety of media he has worked in—painting, drawing, photo-montage, printmaking, and theater design. There's a sense of play here, too. But despite the play, you always know that Hockney's in control; it's distinctively *his* work, whatever the medium.

His early success while still a student in the 1960s quickly carried Hockney into the international arena, where his work met with a mixed response. Some critics see it as merely illustrational. Others appreciate him as a true artist whose work reflects tremendous *joie de vivre.*

The great French painter Henri Matisse (whose influence, incidentally, can be seen in some of Hockney's work), once said that he wanted his art to be like a comfortable armchair, inviting, relaxing, and embracing the viewer. While Hockney's work may seem like a poolside deck chair inviting us to unwind after a hard day on the freeway, the work of Francis Bacon provides such a blow to our nervous system that we may well need an armchair, *any* chair, in which to recover. Bacon occupies the strange position of being both the grand old man and the *enfant terrible* of British art. His large canvasses confront us with contorted figures in enclosed spaces—mortal flesh in convulsion. (It is hard to imagine how a painter of such raw, primal vitality could have been, until his early thirties, an interior designer, but it is interesting to see how the tubular steel furniture so popular in those early days has been transformed into the operating tables and restricting chairs of his paintings.) An inveterate gambler in his work, Bacon employs chance splashes and smears of paint to create a sense of movement, pro-

Tate Gallery

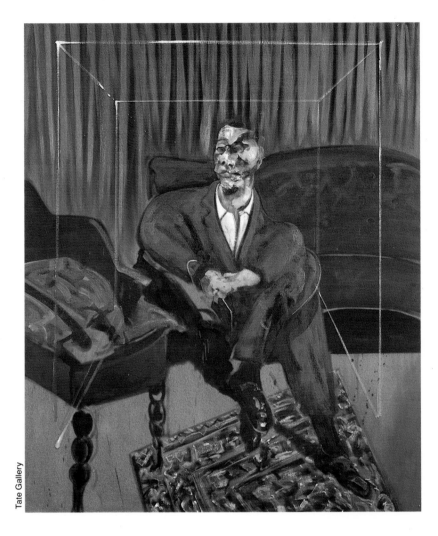

Tate Gallery

viding his despairing subjects with surprising vitality. The violent, poignant urgency here may repel the fainthearted, but there is no denying Bacon's unique, compelling power.

In contrast, the rounded forms of the late sculptor Henry Moore's just barely abstracted works—such as mothers and children, and reclining figures—offer us his vision of a serene world of security and fullness. His simple but stately forms, elemental and maternal, look as if they could have been shaped by the action of the sea, and show his deep imaginative involvement with nature. Despite their massive and robust size and shape, these archetypal forms evoke unexpected feelings of tenderness in the viewer, a desire to stroke the sculptures, to be embraced and protected by them. It is this strong, very basic human connection that could well insure Henry Moore's place as perhaps the most lasting British artist of the twentieth century.

Tate Gallery

Three leading modern British artists of worldwide reputation concentrate on the human form. David Hockney's technical mastery and straightforward pictorial approach to painting are evident in **Mr. and Mrs. Clark and Percy** *(left). The tortured vision prevalent in the works of Francis Bacon can be seen in his painting* **Seated Figure** *(above). Sculptor Henry Moore reduced the human form to elemental shapes that dissolve the boundary between man and nature, as in his* **Maquette for Family Group** *(right).*

Pottery and Porcelain

BRITISH POTTERY AND PORCELAIN is backed by more than two hundred years of tradition. Many of the firms that founded the industry in the eighteenth century are still in operation today, their names synonymous with a variety of styles of fine tableware and porcelain figurines.

Most famous of all, undoubtedly, is Wedgwood, a firm founded in 1759 by Josiah Wedgwood, who to this day is referred to as "the Father of English Potters." Wedgwood was not merely a craftsman; he was an inventor. And his two greatest inventions were most certainly Queen's Ware—a fine cream-colored earthenware developed in 1765 and named for Queen Charlotte, wife of George II—and Jasper, the colored stoneware (usually powder blue) decorated with white classical ornamentation in relief. Indeed, when most people speak of Wedgwood today, it is the blue Jasperware that they are thinking of—even though the many different types of pottery produced by Wedgwood account for approximately a fifth of British ceramic tableware output and one quarter of all exports.

The porcelain made at the Chelsea potteries during their very short period of operation—from 1745 to 1770—is still held to be the best Britain has ever produced. The most typical pieces, prized by collectors to this day, depict shepherds and shepherdesses amid flowering trees. Such pieces were so highly regarded on the Continent that they were widely copied by European manufacturers.

Especially British in design is underglaze painted or printed blue-and-white ware—particularly the "Willow Pattern," first created in England in 1770. The best and rarest early example of this style, however, is Worcester's "Dr. Wall" or "First Period" porcelain, manufactured between 1750 and 1785. Blue-and-white pottery and porcelain has also been produced by, among others, Chaughley, Lowestoft, and Spode.

Tea services understandably rank high in the output of many British potteries. They range widely in style—from the delicate sets of New Hall and heavily patterned Rockingham to the modern streamlined look of Coalport—and are a favorite area of specialization for collectors.

The unsophisticated Staffordshire pottery figure is a delightfully, typically British object. It is the product of a cottage industry, its manufacture spanned the nineteenth century, and is still tremendously popular with collectors. The figures offer a micro-

Josiah Wedgwood & Sons Ltd.

Royal Doulton Ltd.

Sotheby's

British pottery and porcelain range in style from classical to whimsical to strikingly modern. Most classic of all is the powder blue Jasper stoneware made by Wedgwood (left). Pottery figures produced by Royal Doulton (above) are especially popular with collectors. And the Japanese-inspired work of the late Sir Bernard Leach (above right) won acclaim for the modern British craftsman-potter's art.

cosm of British life at that time in their depiction of royalty, heroes and heroines, soldiers, actors and actresses, sportsmen, and so on. Equally British and equally renowned are the jolly, round-faced "Toby" mugs of the eighteenth century, a tradition that has been revived since 1934 in the Toby or character mugs produced by Royal Doulton. Doulton (they became "Royal" in 1901) also issues a myriad selection of figurines, from Art Deco bathing belles and balloon-sellers to "ladies" of all kinds. Devotees of this particular genre come to Britain from all over the world—especially from America—to add to their collections.

British country pottery, with its basic forms and shapes, its soft colors and strong reds and browns, its simple "slip" decorations, has a history dating back to the Middle Ages. It was transformed into somewhat self-conscious "Studio" pottery by the Arts and Crafts Movement of the 1880s. The most famous country-style studio potter of recent years has to be the late Sir Bernard Leach (1887–1979). In 1921, he founded St. Ives Pottery in the Cornish town of the same name. His work, a synthesis of English medieval and Far Eastern forms and decoration—natural clay colors and deep browns embellished with simple, striking brushstrokes—was nothing less than a revolution in the potter's art and had a far-reaching influence both at home and abroad. Leach trained many talented potters, among them William Staite-Murry, one of the most important studio potters to work between the wars. Leach's third wife, Janet, an American, has worked at the Leach pottery in St. Ives since 1956, and his sons have followed in the great man's footsteps: in 1956

David founded Lowderdown Pottery at Bovey Tracey, and Michael, Yelland Manor Pottery, both in Devon; Jeremy started Craft Pottery in London in 1959. David Leach's three sons are also potters. John Leach, who founded Mucheleney Pottery in Somerset in 1964, has developed an international reputation.

Three other twentieth-century British artist-potters are also worth special mention. From 1913 until his death in 1945, William Moorcroft made brightly colored, flower-decorated art pottery now widely sought after. And two women artists, working outside the art and studio traditions, dominated the British Art Deco period of the 1920s and 1930s: Clarice Cliffe with her jazzy shapes and decorations, and Susie Cooper, whose stylized floral and fauna designs (still issued by Wedgwood) are collectors' items.

CHIPPENDALE. SHERATON. Hepplewhite. These three names evoke, in the hearts of lovers of fine furniture, the Golden Age of British eighteenth-century design. But the singular story of British furniture begins long before those glory years, and continues proudly right through the present day.

Up until the sixteenth century, only wealthy Britons could afford good furniture, and then only strong, heavy tables, chests, and a few chairs. Good English oak was the principal wood, used most effectively in the sixteenth and early seventeenth centuries, when the *nouveaux-riches* demanded such grand pieces as sideboards and four-poster beds. The Welsh dresser, of seventeenth-century origin, was a popular cottage piece of the time and now graces

Sotheby's

Furniture:
Its Golden Age to the
Modern Traditionalists

The Crafts Council

many a smartly decorated kitchen or living room.

The real beginning of high-quality British furniture came in 1660, when the "joiner and turner"—essentially a cottage industry workman—was eclipsed by the artist-craftsman cabinetmaker. British furniture soon matched the best of Europe in its design and craftsmanship. It was the Age of Walnut, featuring furniture with veneer, marquetry, and the elegant cabriole leg—a style that came to be associated with Queen Anne (the queen consort, 1702 to 1714).

Around 1750, Thomas Chippendale, the greatest exponent of a light, asymmetric rococo style of furniture, created his mahogany chairs, prized

today as among the ultimate of collector's items. He also perfected two quintessentially British pieces of furniture: the library bookcase and the tea table. By the end of the eighteenth century, Robert Adam had successfully married the seeming frivolity of the rococo style with a more severe classical look in furniture.

Although it is doubtful that any pieces were actually manufactured by them, the designers Sheraton and Hepplewhite gave their names to furniture synonymous with elegance. Pieces designed by them or in their style fit well into modern home interiors, as does much of the furniture of the Regency period—artfully combining, as it often does, the classical

The best of British furniture displays an elegance that transcends time. This is evident in such modern pieces as John Makepeace's graceful three-legged table (bottom left), the high-backed Liverpool bench designed by Ronald Carter (below), and in a Carlton House writing table dating from 1785 (left).

Ronald Carter

look with Egyptian and Chinese motifs. Small-scale Regency and early Victorian papier mâché furniture continues to provide great decorative charm to the modern eye.

The frequently over-large "high" Victorian furniture—particularly pastiche "Gothic," "Renaissance," and "Tudor" styles, is coming back into fashion of late—prized, it seems, as much for its homeliness as for any artistic merit it might have. Some more noteworthy styles of the same period came out of the Arts and Crafts Movement of the 1880s, with its strikingly simple and straightforward designs, and Scottish Art Nouveau, led by Charles Rennie Mackintosh, whose furniture managed at once to be both stark and elaborately decorative. Originals of Mackintosh's excessively high-backed chairs are much in demand, and modern copies of them do a brisk business.

In the 1920s and 1930s, Gordon Russell created restrained and simple furniture for London's Heals department store. The postwar years saw the emergence of Terence Conran (later, Sir Terence), who promoted quality, if not particularly remarkable, furniture in his famous Habitat emporium, at Heals, and in his more upscale Conran's store.

Of late, British furniture seems to be enjoying a new burst of creativity. Much of the credit must go to the designer John Makepeace, whose clean-lined, beautifully crafted furniture seems to take its inspiration from the wood itself. British designers now land big commissions at furniture fairs abroad, and excellent designers are opening new showrooms in London's West End and in Covent Garden. Rodney Kinsman is the best-known designer currently working in the modern idiom; the fact that two of his minimalist chairs are called "Vienna" and "Tokyo" indicates his understanding of the need for British designers to recognize both foreign influences and markets.

Ronald Carter, another important designer, began his career in 1950, and uses mainly English hardwoods to create furniture that owes much to the Arts and Crafts Movement. His best-selling bench, called "Liverpool," with its high back pierced by decorative holes, is a fine example of the sort of handmade furniture that, he avers, "takes the English tradition into the eighties." Another modern traditionalist is Viscount Linley, son of Princess Margaret and Lord Snowdon, who began his own furniture business in 1985. His work, particularly the veneered screens he produces, echo the Age of Walnut in a wholly contemporary manner. As with many things British, the modern age seems merely to have come back full circle to tradition.

Country Crafts

DESPITE, OR PERHAPS BECAUSE of, the fact that the British countryside is diminishing, country crafts are alive and flourishing in modern Britain as never before. Many people are tired of mass-produced goods; they long for something lovingly handmade, and are offering support to craftsmen old and young who are preserving and reviving old skills that were once in danger of disappearing.

Some country crafts, alas, *have* gone. There is little use for the expertise of the wheelwright, who was once one of the most important men in any village. Often serving as his neighbors' woodsman, carpenter, and blacksmith, he was principally responsible for constructing sturdy farm wagons with huge iron-rimmed wheels—vehicles now largely confined to folk museums. Nor will you be able to find a dry-stone waller to construct a wall of carefully chosen stones fitted together with almost jigsaw-puzzle-like precision without aid of cement. Though their profession may no longer be in demand, the walls they built in the Yorkshire Dales, on the moors of Devonshire

BTA

BTA

Many old-fashioned country crafts continue to thrive in modern Britain. The art of the thatcher (left) is still much in need to maintain the thatched roofs of traditional cottages such as the one above, which belonged to Shakespeare's wife, Anne Hathaway. Weavers and tapestry makers such as those at the Edinburgh Tapestry Company (right), who design and make modern pieces, are finding ready markets for their wares.

The Edinburgh Tapestry Company Ltd.

and Cornwall, and in the Cotswolds were so well constructed that they are now and will remain a pleasant feature of the British landscape for centuries to come.

Until recently, it was thought that the ancient craft of thatching had died, too—a pity, since the thatched cottage roof is one of the glories of the British countryside. But many Britons are now actively buying and preserving old country cottages, with a resulting resurgence in demand for the thatcher's skills, while the British Master Thatchers' Association now offers courses to aspiring newcomers to the craft.

Throughout Britain, the love of horse-riding ensures that the ringing of hammer on anvil at the blacksmith's forge is still heard; and it rings even more with the repair of iron farm implements and a new interest in traditional and modern wrought-ironwork. Old village crafts such as carpentry, spinning, dyeing, weaving, and pottery all thrive. Modern versions of Welsh loving spoons —ornately carved gifts made by young men for their lady-loves—are still popular gift-shop items. And at harvest time, all over Britain, straw is still fashioned into the age-old corn dollies that children love.

Much of such activity today is fostered by the Crafts Council of Great Britain. At its headquarters in Waterloo Place, near Piccadilly in London, visitors can view touring exhibitions on British crafts, buy books, and gather information. The council also gives grants to promising craftsmen, forms guilds, and generally promotes fine craftsmanship. Another organization, the Council for Small Industries in Rural Areas (CoSIRA), has been largely responsible for setting up some fifty craft centers throughout Britain. Many of these are housed in restored farm buildings, mills, and breweries that might otherwise have

disappeared and consist of a number of workshops where craftsmen ply their trades and offer goods for sale.

The importance of crafts to Britain's heritage won its most serious recognition in 1975, when the Victoria and Albert Museum in London held a very successful exhibition, "The Craftsman's Art," to celebrate the opening of the V&A Craft Council Shop. Today, a number of modern craft pieces are included in the museum's world-class collection, further proof that its country crafts may well rank as one of Britain's finest and most enduring contributions to the world of decorative arts.

Chapter 10
Fashion

OF ALL NATIONAL SYMBOLS, TAR-tan may well be the world's most widely recognized; fashioned into clothing worldwide and into a range of traditional garments at home, this Scottish cloth is certainly the most used and useful of symbols. In Gaelic, it is called *braecan*, meaning particolored or speckled (the word *tartan* comes from the French *tire-taine*, meaning a coarse fabric of wool and linen or cotton). It is a plaid cloth made of different colored wools woven into a distinctive pattern of stripes and checks—known techni-cally as the "sett"—by which a par-ticular clan, family, or regiment is as-sociated or identified.

Few Scots, or those of Scottish descent, fail to be stirred by the tar-tan. A symbol of patriotism, it keeps alive a spirit of loyalty to the clan and to Scotland's romantic past. Its ori-gins, however, are lost in the mists of the Scottish Highlands. Variously pat-terned cloaks, kilts, and "trews" (trou-sers) were worn by Highland peas-ants and clan chiefs alike since earliest times. King James V of Scot-land is known to have worn a suit of tartan in 1538, and to this day British royalty makes a show of wearing it on appropriate occasions. When the Royal Family visits Scotland to attend the Braemar Games every August, its members wear the Balmoral tartan, a pattern designed around 1848 by Prince Albert, Queen Victoria's con-sort. Another tartan, Royal Stuart, is exclusive to the British sovereign, though eight other Scottish families are entitled to wear variations of the Stuart (or Stewart) sett.

The present popularity tartan en-joys, along with all things Scottish, is due to a number of significant histor-ical factors. When Bonnie Prince Charlie made his abortive bid for the British throne in 1745, a legendary Scottish figure was born. The atten-tion of Britons nationwide was fo-cused on Scotland. Things Scottish became fashionable, romantic, and, of course, commercial. In time, an enterprising Edinburgh tailor was ad-vertising tartans "in the newest pat-terns." Such enterprise swelled the ranks of tartan setts from only fifty-five in 1831 to approximately one thousand today.

Tartan's growing popularity suf-fered a setback in 1747 when Parlia-ment passed the Dress Act, making its wearing illegal. But by the time the Act was repealed in 1783, a Celtic re-vival was already in the air. The publi-cation of the last of Sir Walter Scott's "Waverly Novels" in 1819 increased the romantic view of Highland life. Fi-nally, King George IV gave it his ap-proval when he wore Royal Stuart to a reception at Holyrood House in 1822.

Further royal approval came in 1855 when, on a visit to Scotland, Queen Victoria fell in love with the

Wearing the Colors of the Clan

Camera Press, London

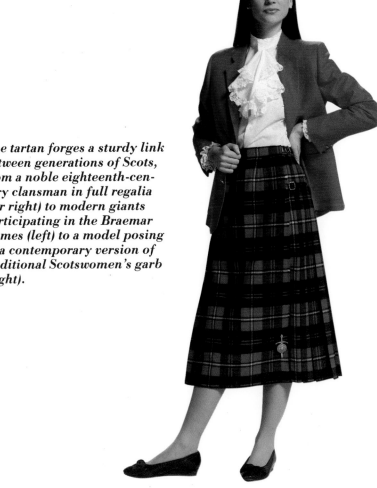

The tartan forges a sturdy link between generations of Scots, from a noble eighteenth-century clansman in full regalia (far right) to modern giants participating in the Braemar Games (left) to a model posing in a contemporary version of traditional Scotswomen's garb (right).

Kinloch Anderson Ltd.

Scottish National Portrait Gallery

country. Soon, Prince Albert's Balmoral Castle was resplendent with tartan carpets, sofas, and chairs. Tartan became the fabric of choice for many a Victorian crinoline.

Today, tartan garments continue to be an accepted form of dress in Scotland. At Highland meetings and annual balls, men don the kilt and women wear tartan sashes, secured by brooches, over their left shoulders. In addition, every Scottish regiment of Britain's army has its own official sett. The most famous regi-

mental tartan, and still the most popular with the public at large, is that of the Black Watch. A bold pattern of black and green, it now appears on everything from luggage to all manner of Scottish souvenirs.

For men, the kilt—a full, pleated "skirt" that ends just above the knee—is always custom-tailored. The effect is extremely dashing, and wearers find the garment warm and practical. Traditionally, nothing is worn underneath—though no self-respecting Scotsman will admit it.

Women's kilts are cut somewhat less fully than men's. Properly speaking, they are known as tartan skirts and are usually sold off the rack.

People are often confused by the difference between "dress" tartan and "hunting" tartan. Dress tartan always has a white base and traditionally is worn only by women. Hunting tartan, as its name implies, is appropriate wear when out shooting game; its browns, greens, grays, and blues are perfect camouflage among the heather and the lochs.

Strictly speaking, tartan of any sort can only be worn by those who claim the historical right, those who are members, in other words, of a particular Scottish clan. But the Scots are a generous people, and they also know a good source of tourist trade when they see one. Today anyone can buy a length of tartan material, wear a tartan scarf or tie, carry tartan-patterned luggage, or even, emulating Prince Albert, decorate an entire room with the tartan of his or her fancy.

The Country Look

FROM THE OLD ARISTOCRACY AND gentry who lived in, hunted in, supported, and farmed it, to the present-day town-dweller with his or her rustic weekend cottage, the British have enjoyed a centuries-long love affair with their countryside, a preoccupation that is distinctively displayed in a particularly British style of clothing.

Apart from such obvious garments as old and easy-fitting casual suits, sports jackets, pullovers, coats, skirts, and macintoshes, a number of garments are especially designed for and suited to the country. Many of them, not surprisingly, have a sporting origin. The short, lightweight Covert coat and the oiled-cotton Barbour jacket are popular for fishing, shooting, and riding. Country men sport military sweaters with leather-patched shoulders and elbows, and cavalry twill trousers—comfortable, sensible clothes to protect them from the elements. Likewise, country women wear their Hermes scarves and good "sensible" brogues for rambling. In the saddle, both sexes wear hand-tailored cloth riding breeches and shop-bought cord breeches in brown or Loden green; duffle coats and flat caps when spectators at point-to-point races. There are hunting and hiking boots, deer-stalker hats (à la Sherlock Holmes), and, of course, tweed jackets.

Tweed—no material evokes the sense of the countryside better. The word is Scottish in origin, a corruption of *tweel* or *twill*, referring to the diagonal weave that is the basis of

Kinloch Anderson Ltd.

The country look embraces many traditional styles, from richly textured Scottish fisherman's knit sweaters (left) to Laura Ashley fashions (right) that evoke a nostalgic English world of rural picnics and high tea taken in the open air.

Courtesy of Laura Ashley

these heavy-duty fabrics with six centuries of tradition behind them. Tweed is also associated with the River Tweed, dividing Scotland from England, and by extension with the lands to the north, renowned for their tweed-weaving industry.

Tweed was originally used as a "plaid"—that is, a rectangular length of cloth wrapped loosely over the shoulder as an outer garment. The earliest cloths were of small black-and-white checks, which evolved into a pattern now known as District Checks. Many of today's patterns date from the nineteenth century, when rich hunting sportsmen from the South frequented the Scottish Highlands. Wishing to distinguish

and separate their retainers from native sheepmen, they added brightly colored checks to the local patterns, resulting in more than a hundred different tweeds.

The most famous Scottish tweeds today are Glenurquhart, closely followed by Harris—cloths that are always hand-woven. Popular patterns include Glenclub Check, Invarary, and the heather-colored Lovat tweed, most of which are known, because of the relative subtlety of their patterns, as "common" twills. Tweed wears extraordinarily well, and it is not uncommon for jackets made of the cloth to last for decades—a significant factor in the fame tweed enjoys.

Equally intrinsic to the British

country look is woolen knitwear. Cashmere, a luxurious blend of Tibetan and Mongolian wools, understandably heads the list. Imported into Scotland, the wool is dyed, spun, and woven into some of the world's most coveted garments. Lambswool knitwear is made primarily from imported wools from Australia, while Shetland is fashioned from the finest British wools. Among the most popular kinds of country knitwear are the intricately patterned and colored Fair Isle sweaters, the best of which are hand-knitted in the northernmost islands of Scotland, and the cream-colored Aran sweaters long-favored by fishermen, with their complicated braidlike patterns.

For many people today, the British country look is synonymous with the clothing designed and sold by the late Laura Ashley. She began with a small attic business in 1953. Using natural fabrics (at first, only one-hundred-percent cotton) in delicate floral designs, Ashley aimed to revive and evoke through her clothing (and later in a line of furnishing fabrics and wallcoverings) the sense of idyllic romance that is the essence of the English countryside, allowing her customers to enjoy the delights of rural life wherever they live. With more than 180 Laura Ashley shops throughout the world today, one could say that the English country look has gone global.

The Cutting Edge of Fashion

Modern British designers exhibit flair, daring, and high style. Bruce Oldfield's dramatic evening outfit is a study in textural contrast (left) with its sculpted leather jacket and gossamer-thin skirt. Zandra Rhodes decks two very feminine dresses (right) with dazzling sequins. Betty Jackson's oversized, boldly patterned outfits (far right) make a brash yet elegant statement.

DURING THE LATE 1950s AND THE first years of the 1960s, anyone referrring to the "cutting edge" of British fashion was most likely making a punning reference to dressmaking scissors forged from Sheffield steel. British fashion had no innovative impact. Between the chain stores, in the first throes of their love affair with synthetic fabrics, and such couture houses as Hartnell and Hardy Amies churning out their dull daywear and blowsy ballgowns for dwindling ranks of debs, there lay a vast wasteland.

But the 1960s witnessed a revolution that was to change the face of British fashion. It was a revolution triggered by the emergence of a whole new generation of Britons, British teenagers. Previously, the teens, like toothaches and contagious childhood diseases, had been an affliction to be borne, that tedious bridge between the well-defined fashion statements of ankle socks and Mum's sensible suits. Then two names came along to fill the gap—Mary Quant and Barbara Hulanicki. Almost single-handedly, these two designers lifted British fashion from the morass of watered-down imitations of Parisian catwalks (Milan, at this particular point in history, being rather too avant garde for the British); they gave it an identity that was utterly unique, albeit idiosyncratic.

Suddenly, fashion was no longer the exclusive province of the middle-aged middle classes, whose affluence had heretofore granted them instant chic. Now fashion was the inheritance of the young working woman willing to sacrifice her hard-earned cash at the altar of style. Under the guidance of Quant and Hulanicki, fashion became fun, a means of self-expression that was neither necessarily radical nor conservative, merely individual.

Little matter then that the boutiques that stocked their designs proved as ephemeral as the clothes themselves, the miniskirts, maxiskirts, see-through blouses, and psychadelia. The important thing was that for the first time, fashion had been transported from the realm of dictatorship; women found themselves emancipated. And out of the ashes of early pop fashion's defunct revolution there rose an entirely new generation of serious British designers destined to take their places alongside the St. Laurents and Armanis of the fashion world.

Perhaps the most direct descendent of the 1960s movement is Katharine Hamnett, high priestess of radical chic. For her, clothes are a sexual and a political statement: "People buy clothes to get laid," she is on record as having said. And

Christopher Bissell

what." The end results may vary, but the approach is a united one, designing clothes that flatter British women's bodies as they are, hips and all; the hallmarks are simplicity, excellent cut, and outstanding workmanship, all at realistic prices. The tradition of great British tailoring is unmistakable in Conran's tuxedos, slick city suits, and gored skirts, or in Oldfield's elegantly sensuous evening wear. Wendy Dagworthy and Betty Jackson's circular skirts, oversized shirts, and easy dresses may seem less formally structured, but their stylish, fluid lines rely just as much on craftsmanship as Conran's does.

Simple craft aside, all fashion is ultimately an art of illusion, an elaborate fantasy enabling us to change personality, chameleon-like, at will. And no designer understands this

spell-weaving better than Zandra Rhodes and David and Elizabeth Emanuel. For them, extravagance and femininity are not at odds with the austerity and the feminism of the 1980s. Rather, they're alternative facets. When a woman wears a vibrant, sequinned Zandra Rhodes creation, she becomes an exotic bird of paradise. In a demure, frilled Emanuel gown, she assumes the guise of a fairy-tale princess (no wonder this husband-and-wife team made Princess Di's wedding gown). And so what if that same woman chooses to wear a double-breasted suit with slacks and a man's tie tomorrow. It was only when the nation's designers finally came to realize that women demanded this kind of freewheeling freedom that the cutting edge of British fashion was truly honed.

whether that means seducing the boyfriend, the boss, the bank manager, or the voter, it all amounts to the same thing. The controversial "58% don't want Pershing" T-shirt Hamnett wore to meet Prime Minister Margaret Thatcher in 1982 (protesting the presence of American Pershing missiles in Britain) was typically uncompromising. And significantly, Hamnett is prepared to put her money where her slogans are; a per-

centage of the proceeds from sales of her T-shirts goes to charity.

Combative politics are not the issue for Jaspar Conran (son of designer Sir Terence and pop novelist Shirley), Betty Jackson, Wendy Dagworthy, Bruce Oldfield, and a host of others. What *is* at issue for them is the way women live in the 1980s. Conran seems to speak for them all when he says, "I make clothes for the woman who works, no matter at

The Princess Di Look

PRINCESS DIANA IS THE FEAR-less, undisputed leader of the British fashion world. And where she leads, the British rag trade is swift to ensure that the consumer follows—whether it be in the direction of spotty ankle socks, net bows on the heels of tights, or feathered tricorn hats. A princess by marriage, Diana is by public appointment an international cover girl.

Yet, as recently as 1980, Lady Diana Spencer—as she then was known—was just another upper-class teenager, or, as self-appointed style commentator Peter York would have it, a Sloane Ranger (a term coined for that class of "gells" who frequent the shops along Sloane Street in London). Her clothes were the uniform of her age group and social class. In town, she wore casual, colorful shirts, pants and sweaters from the Italian chain store Bennetton, romantic floral skirts and blouses with frilled collars from Laura Ashley, occasional Marks and Spencer knits, and ethnic glamour from Monsoon for the evening. Weekends in the country found her in the obligatory buckled green Hunter Wellingtons (only the British could elevate a waterproof rubber boot to a status symbol—only they would need to), warding off the cold in jolly Peruvian sweaters topped by a Puffa waistcoat (surely the most unflattering garment known to womankind, and undoubtedly inspired by the inflated little Michelin tire man, with his numerous "rolls" of rubber-fat).

Once the engagement became official in February 1981, the media bloodhounds, already hot on the scent, closed in for the kill, and Diana's days of diaphanous cotton skirts were strictly numbered. At only nineteen years of age, she was faced with the daunting prospect of creating her own royal image. And while she was prepared to be guided by the Queen and Queen Mother in matters of protocol, Diana was determined not to succumb to their frankly staid sense of fashion. Any speculation to the contrary was instantly dispelled by the disclosure that the royal bride's wedding dress would be made by a young, virtually unknown husband-and-wife design team, David and Elizabeth Emanuel.

Though independent, Diana was certainly not rash, and she was as-tute enough to realize that the instinctive fashion sense that had carried her through the courtship would be inadequate for her new role. Beatrix Miller, then editor-in-chief of British *Vogue* and an acknowledged fashion expert, was enlisted to advise the fledgling princess on every aspect of clothes and makeup. It was Miller who fostered Diana's catholic taste in designers (something of a necessity, since she was, for the best patriotic reasons, restricted to British contenders). Everyone from Belville Sassoon to Benny Ong was assessed as a potential contributor to the royal wardrobe, and John Boyd was recommended as milliner. A thorough teacher, Beatrix Miller analyzed her pupil's progress during appointments Diana kept by sneaking up the back staircase of Condé Nast headquarters to her mentor's office. Even today, the Princess of Wales relies on Miller's guidance.

Inevitably, the transformation from girl-about-town to princess was not effortlessly smooth. In the early days there were plenty of mistakes. Over-fussy necklines, hats worn with all the gaucherie of one unaccustomed to them, and, of course, that black décolleté Emanuel evening gown Diana wore to the opera—a garment that overstepped the tenuous bounds of decorum and was said not to have amused the Queen. Then, too, there was the wedding dress; it was marvelous in the fitting room, but unfortunately no one had considered the devastation that could be wreaked by

Snowdon/Camera Press, London

Camera Press, London

bundling a landing strip of delicate silk into a glass coach.

Diana, for her part, was an eager pupil. Gradually, the mistakes became fewer and fewer. And as she has developed from a slightly chubby teenager into a slender, beautiful woman (not, it must be added, without a great deal of effort), her style has grown more poised and assured. The hairstyle that launched a thousand pairs of scissors now has a softer, fuller look and blonder, more flattering highlights. The fussy frills and flounces have been replaced by sleeker lines. Reminders of her earlier favorites—the jewel-bright reds and fuschias and blues she loves to wear, and the low-heeled pumps to minimize her height next to Charles —are still apparent. But nowadays they are worn with that distinctive, Diana touch: a string of pearls knotted backward over a plunging backless dress, matching colored tights, or a pair of jaunty shoe bows.

Against all the odds, Diana has managed to remain an individual.

And in doing so, she has succeeded in securing a place quite unique in the nation's affections. Her style, within the obvious constraints imposed upon her by her station, is often recognizably in sync with her contemporaries. Many a long-suffering father or boyfriend sympathized with Prince Charles when his wife attended a pop concert wearing his tuxedo, jazzed up with a cummerbund. Once again, the Princess Di look had set the press rocking all over the world.

Camera Press, London

Patrick Lichfield/Camera Press, London

Princess Diana has single-handedly done more to promote British fashion than any other person in history. Her classic beauty (displayed at its best in the Lord Snowdon portrait shown opposite), provides the most talented designers with a perfect foil. Before her wedding, she was rather ordinarily sporty (above). But from the moment she appeared in her bridal gown (left), designed by the Emmanuels, she made fashion news with every outfit. The Princess Di look continues to evolve (right) with her continued flair for millinery as she herself grows more mature and self-assured.

Chapter 11
Sports

The Derby and Royal Ascot

YOU CANNOT SPEAK OF HORSE racing in Britain without mentioning the name of Lester Pigott. Now retired, he was eighteen times the top—or joint-top—jockey at Royal Ascot. He first won the nation's premier classic, the Derby, on Never Say Die in 1954, and continued riding Derby winners through the 1960s, 1970s, and well into the 1980s. In all, Pigott rode twenty-nine "Classics." For thirty years, he was an integral part of the British horse-racing scene—especially at Ascot, which in his opinion stages the best horse race in the country, the King George VI and Queen Elizabeth Diamond Stakes. Pigott has won it seven times.

Despite Pigott's opinion, the Derby, inaugurated by the second Earl of Derby on May 4th, 1780, is still the major horse-racing event for most people. Benjamin Disraeli described it as "the Blue Riband of the Turf." On a quiet day, the Epsom Downs course in Surrey, on London's southwestern fringe, may look a bit tatty. But on Derby day, now the first Wednesday in June, it is transformed into a veritable carnival. Down on the Downs themselves, ordinary bettors —"punters," as they are called—have their fortunes told by gypsies and bet and carouse as they have done for centuries. Up in the smart boxes of the grandstands, "society"—men in

morning suits and gray top hats, women in whatever current fashion decrees—takes its pleasures more sedately. In the nineteenth century, the Derby was such a mandatory day out for the ruling classes that the Houses of Parliament closed down and members of both the Lords and the Commons decamped to Epsom for the races. Both Parliament and

racing have changed since then, and now very few members maintain an interest in horseflesh. For the most part, racing today is dominated by foreigners like the Aga Khan and the Maktoum family.

The most notable exception to this change, however, is Her Majesty the Queen, for whom racing has always been an abiding passion. She

has had more than two dozen horses in training at one time. If you study royal photographs, you will see that the only occasions on which the Queen allows herself to display real emotion in public is when she is watching a race.

Royal Ascot is where she is most on display, riding to the course from Windsor Castle in an open carriage

Colorsport

Colorsport

Katalin Arkell

Three traditional aspects of British racing: the great Lester Pigott (left), riding to victory in a race in October 1985; the Queen arriving at the Royal Enclosure at Ascot; and a young Briton posing at Royal Ascot (right).

drawn by four gray horses with postilions in court dress and wigs. This race, held during the third week of June, was inaugurated by Queen Anne in 1711, when it was more or less a private affair for the court. Later that century, the public was admitted—but only on sufferance.

It is still a little like that. For those who want to gain admittance to the Queen's presence, the Royal Enclosure is not only the best place from which to see the event but also the best place to be seen. About ten thousand people can cram in, and they even allow divorcees—not an acceptable practice in the early years of the Queen's reign. Ladies are, however, still required to wear hats in the enclosure, a fact that gives rise to frequent argument. Her Majesty's representative, the Marquess of Abergavenny (pronounced, of course, "Abergenny") rules on matters of dress, and change does not seem likely to be forthcoming. However, Ascot hats are at least notable for their flamboyance. As the marquess's secretary was once heard to remark on the subject, "How many flowers go to make a hat?"

Royal Ascot today is full of starlets showing off their hats and themselves for the TV cameras, and of businessmen entertaining clients on their expense accounts. But it still has a certain cachet and class. It always has, ever since the day Queen Victoria was driven over in a coach and advised by her prime minister, Lord Melbourne, on no account to place a bet. It would, he advised, "destroy the grandeur of the race." It would appear the grandeur of the Royal Ascot remains unimpaired to this day.

IF RACING IS THE SPORT OF Kings, then polo—basically a game of hockey played on horseback—is the Pastime of Princes. The princes in this case are Charles, Prince of Wales, and his father, Philip, Duke of Edinburgh. Their enthusiasm for the sport was passed on to them by their late "Uncle Dickie" Mountbatten, who was not technically a prince but always looked like one—a haughty Battenberg aristocrat who so loved dressing up in the uniform of Admiral of the Fleet, with all his innumerable medals and decorations, that it sometimes seemed as if a particularly handsome Christmas tree had miraculously taken on human form.

Lord Mountbatten was not only a keen player but a student of the game. Under the pseudonym "Marco" (a pun, as in "Marco Polo"), he wrote a prewar textbook on the game that is still widely regarded as the standard work. His nephew, Prince Philip, became a very keen player with a reputation for aggression, fearlessness, bad language, and indifference to his ponies' welfare. Philip's son Prince Charles seems just as keen on the playing field (despite critics' assertions that he was bullied into the game by his macho dad, who thinks Chuck's a wimp); but he is nicer to the horses, and generally more polite.

Major Ronnie Ferguson, who used to play alongside Philip and now manages Charles' polo, is fond of saying that everyone is equal on the polo field, whether a royal or not. The only difference is that your expletives should include an occasional "sir," as in, "What the bloody hell do you think you're doing, sir?" when addressing royalty. Some, as George Orwell said, are more equal than others. Ferguson is, after all, an ex-

Polo and the Hunt

Colorsport

Camera Press, London

Prince Charles displayed keen enthusiasm and skill in polo matches played on a visit to the United States (far left) and in a match played at home at Smith's Lawn in Windsor (left).

Huntsmen (right), some of them wearing the bright scarlet jackets known as hunting pink, set out on a chilly morning in pursuit of the elusive and cunning fox.

Katalin Arkéll

officer of the Household Cavalry, and now Prince Andrew's father-in-law.

The royals play most of their polo at Windsor, close to the castle. The ground is known as Smith's Lawn and is the home of the Guards' Polo Club. Though the game is full of retired majors like Ferguson, many of the Guards' Club members have nothing to do with the army. What they do have—unlike most majors— is money. There are Greek shipowners, Swiss bankers, and a German industrialist named Christian Heppe, who presented the ground with its royal box and is a Life Member of the club. The high point of the polo year comes in August, when Cartier, the jewelers, sponsor an "International Day" pitting England against a for-

eign team for the Coronation Cup. Prince Charles usually plays in the backfield on England's second squad or "B" team.

Besides Guards', other smart polo clubs can be found at Cowdray Park in Sussex, home of Lord Cowdray, who was largely responsible for reviving the game after the war; and at Cirencester, where the driving force is the Vestey family, whose considerable fortunes derive from Argentine beef. (Argentina has been a dodgy subject in the British polo world since the Falklands War of 1982, and particularly embarrassing because the "Argies" have always produced most of the game's best players and ponies.) By way of contrast to these established clubs, a brand new polo club

was opened in 1986 by Bryan Morrison, the music publisher of the now-defunct pop group Wham! More lavishly appointed than the rather spartan older clubs, it is called the Royal County of Berkshire Polo Club, a grand title designed to obscure its lack of age and breeding. The Pastime of Princes marches on.

In winter, the off-season for polo, many players, including Prince Charles, take to the hunting field— "the unspeakable in full pursuit of the uneatable," as Oscar Wilde described it. Despite increasingly violent opposition from many animal rights activists, fox hunting appears to be as popular as ever in Britain. The most fashionable hunts are the Quorn held in Leicestershire and the Beaufort

(much patronized by the Royal Family) held in the Cotswolds. Like polo, the hunt tends to be quite an expensive sport, what with the horses, hounds, and uniforms. Hunting pink is still *de rigeur*, though like so many British customs it is not quite what it seems to be. The "pink" in this case refers to the bright scarlet of the huntsmen's jackets, and the term is thought to have come about as a way to distinguish the riders' garments from the bright red coats worn by British soldiers well into the nineteenth century. Yet, as far as many British animal rights activists are concerned today, anyone in hunting pinks is no better than a soldier of an invading army, threatening the lives of the nation's woodland creatures.

Thames River Sports

THERE HAS BEEN A REGATTA AT Henley-on-Thames every year since 1839, when it was decided that it "would not only be productive of the most beneficial results to the town of Henley, but from its peculiar attractions would also be a source of amusement and gratification to the neighbourhood and to the public in general." These Victorian aspirations seem to have been vindicated. Nowadays, at least fifty thousand spectators converge every year on the river banks during the first week of July to drink champagne, eat smoked salmon and strawberries, and occasionally watch young, athletic oarsmen from all over the world power past them toward the finish line located just short of the Henley Bridge and the graceful tower of the Henley parish church.

More than almost any other event on the English summer calendar, Henley confuses sport and society. No one knows whether it is one of the great sporting events in the social season or one of the great social events in the sporting one. Not that the question greatly taxes anyone.

Although it has been the scene of the rowing events at two Olympic games, the course is no longer up to modern Olympic standards because it has only two lanes and is not on still water. But this doesn't seem to

Katalin Arkell

Colorsport

On the Thames during the Henley Regatta, spectators celebrate the event in traditional dress, including flowing gowns and elaborate hats for the women (left) and, for the men, vividly striped blazers complete with boutonniers and club emblems (above right), bowties or striped club ties, straw boater hats or snap-brims, white or cream flannel trousers with matching shoes, and perhaps the additional flourish of a walking stick. Crews of four, rather than the traditional eight, compete along a placid stretch of the Thames (above).

Katalin Arkell

prevent Harvard and Yale from sending their "eights"—crews of eight men—to compete in the Grand Challenge Cup, nor any number of Olympic oarsmen in the Diamond Sculls or the Thames Challenge.

On land, the Henley Regatta is one of those rare occasions when male fashion vies with female in ostentation. The stewards of the event have a strict dress code, and the secretary will throw people out of the enclosure if they offend. The standards to which spectators must adhere were once described by Princess Alexandra as "gay formal," meaning, in practice, that chaps who really want to cut a dash should wear white or cream flannel trousers, a striped blazer and striped necktie—both in the brightest colors imaginable—and a straw boater hat with a striped ribbon in a bold color.

The smartest color, appropriately enough, is a smoked-salmon/strawberries-and-cream pink—the distinguishing hue of Britain's grandest rowing club, Leander, whose clubhouse is near the entrance to the enclosure. In the sleek but ancient motor launches that tail the racing crews and carry huge banners saying UMPIRE, you will invariably see elderly gentlemen in the club's trademark fluorescent pink caps, standing up in the bows on the lookout for technical infringements.

Britain's other great rowing event also originally finished at Henley Bridge, but is now rowed over four miles and 374 yards of distinctly choppy tidal river in metropolitan London between Putney and Mortlake. Described with characteristic terseness as simply "the Boat Race," it is the annual aquatic struggle between Oxford and Cambridge Universities. Because it is rowed in March, the weather is nearly always freezing cold, unlike that for the Henley Regatta, which can be almost warm. Nevertheless, the Boat Race still attracts large crowds, live television coverage, and as much national interest as any sporting event of the year.

For years, the race was dominated by the Light Blues, as the Cambridge crew is known; but in recent times there has been a Dark Blue (Oxford) ascendancy of almost embarrassing proportions—stemmed by a Cambridge victory in 1986. In spite of its obvious symbolic importance as a battle between the nation's two greatest institutions of learning, the Boat Race is usually quite a boring little spectacle—nothing more than a straightforward procession by the time the crews reach the mile post. It is best watched from the terrace of one of the riverside pubs or at one of the parties given by owners of riverside homes along the course in the London suburbs of Hammersmith or Barnes. With luck, your hosts will have an open fire and a television set so you need only glance briefly, drink in hand, at the real thing as it swirls past just outside the window.

FOREIGNERS WATCHING ALFRED Hitchcock's 1938 movie, *The Lady Vanishes,* in which two pukka Englishmen called Charters and Caldicott can think of nothing but the England versus Australia cricket score, assume the characters are exaggerated. Not so. For generations of Englishmen, cricket was life itself. Nowadays, the game does not oc-

lebone Cricket Club), distinguished by their uniquely shrill neckties of gold and orange, known locally as "rhubarb and custard"; the youthful players of the sport; the modern Getty-financed "Mound" grandstand; the elegant Victorian pavilion. Every year, Lord's is the scene of at least one "Test" match against a foreign touring team, as well as host of the

domestic cup finals and such charming anachronisms as the Eton and Harrow school match and the Oxford and Cambridge University contest.

More recently, Lord's has also become the venue for a village cup final. "Village" cricket is the apotheosis of this English sport. Venture out into the English countryside on a summer weekend and you will still

Life Itself: Cricket

cupy quite the pivotal role in *la vie Anglaise* as it did between the wars, but it indisputably remains the national sport.

Few games have so permeated a nation's life as cricket has England's. If a chap offends the unwritten code of behavior of an English officer and gentleman, his fellow chaps will say, sternly, "Not cricket!" Nothing could be more damning. If life gets difficult for an Englishman, he is said to be "playing on a sticky wicket." The only way to counter such adversity is with "a straight bat." And so on.

The headquarters of cricket is Lord's Cricket Ground, in the St. John's Wood neighborhood of London, where they have been playing the game consistently since 1814. The ground's name has nothing to do with lords and ladies, but is simply the name of the place's first proprietor, a Yorkshireman called Thomas Lord. Like so much of England, Lord's is the backdrop for an extremely odd mixture of ancient and modern: the ancient members of M.C.C. (the initials that are usually employed when referring to the Mary-

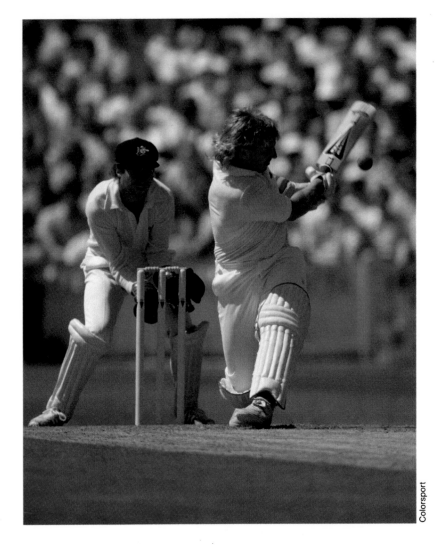

English cricket star Ian Botham displays impeccable style and expertise batting against Australia at Trent Bridge with Australian Wayne Philips catching (left) and bowling against the same team (above).

Colorsport

find "flannelled fools" clad in long white trousers and shirts and sweaters—eleven per side, two willow "bats" at a time, and one leather ball. With luck, there will be a classic backdrop to the scene: an English pub, an English country house, and an English parish church.

The game itself is a constant, slow-motion flux of pace and pitch, but, like a revered American pastime, is essentially a contest between one man who propels a sphere at another man wielding a wooden stick. Armed with that basic knowledge, you can begin to enjoy watching the game, even though there are infinite complexities that make cricket unfathomably mysterious to the outsider—but which reveal themselves, like all good things, with time.

"First class" or professional cricket is played by seventeen English counties throughout the summer. "Championship" league games take no more than a single day. Real pur-

ists hate these, regarding them as ersatz games. They prefer the five-day "Test Matches" between England and one of the former colonial countries to whom the British originally taught the game. Best of all for these stalwarts are the games played against Australia for the "Ashes." These, preserved in a funereal urn, are reputed to be the burned remains of the wooden bats used during England's first-ever defeat by their oldest foreign opponent, and commemorate "The Death of English Cricket."

Before the last world war, "Test Matches" were often "timeless"—that is, they went on for as long as it took for a clear winner to emerge, often seemingly forever. Nowadays, if time runs out the game may be declared a draw, though it still sometimes seems without end. Frequently, however, the English climate will still, as in so many things, have the last word, and the match ceases with the bald announcement: "Rain stopped play."

Good sportsmanship is fundamental to the game of cricket. Members of the Middlesex Cricket Club give a heartfelt round of applause to Australian batter Alan Border at Lord's Cricket Ground (below left). And English captain David Gower proudly holds the Ashes after England's victory over Australia in 1985.

Colorsport

Colorsport

ALL OVER THE WORLD, WHEREVER anyone chases a ball across a golf course, they are strolling through a transplanted piece of Scotland.

Though other countries may claim to have invented it, the game of golf is a distinctly Scottish phenomenon. The Chinese say it evolved from *Ch'ui Wan,* a "ball-hitting game" more than two thousand years old. Romans played a similar game, *paganica,* which they may well have

target or goal was needed at which to direct such projectiles, and rabbit holes were very likely the first cups golfers aimed for.

It was a short step to a more organized form of the pastime. Placement of the cups was no longer left to the whim of rabbits, and golfers began to organize a succession of different holes following the unique terrain of each particular linksland. Though today's championship

The Sport of the Linksland

brought with them to Britain in the fourth century A.D. The Belgians and the Dutch can point to evidence that the game existed in their countries more than six hundred years ago.

Scotland, however, holds the soundest proof that golf is *their* sport. And that proof lies in the land itself—namely, the Scottish linksland. A combination of high sand dunes, dense prickly scrublands, naturally eroded bunkers, and lush grassy hollows, linkslands formed naturally around the estuaries of the great Scottish rivers—notably those of the Forth, Eden, and Tay. These were public lands, perfect for healthy rambling walks, and more than six hundred years ago Scotsmen began to develop the pastime of carrying a stick along with them on such walks, using it to bat stones—and later, feather balls—ahead of them. Soon a

courses are a standardized eighteen holes, the number at early golf links varied with the location: those at the Scottish town of Leith, for example, had only five, while the Montrose links had twenty-five.

The most notable early golf course, and still one of the world's most famous, is located in the linksland of St. Andrews. Golf was played there as early as 1414. Founded in 1754, the Society of St. Andrews Golfers was the second golfing club in Britain (followed ten years later by the Honourable Company of Edinburgh Golfers at Leith, a club that disbanded in 1831). At St. Andrews, for the first time ever, man began to help nature, carefully planning and altering the links to introduce deliberate hazards and opportunities for strategy in the game. The St. Andrews course was reorganized and set at eighteen holes (the reason —surely apocryphal—being that there are eighteen jiggers in a bottle of Scotch whisky, a jigger per hole for every player who carried a bottle).

In 1834, the St. Andrews links were recognized as being "Royal and Ancient" by King William IV. The appellation was also tacked onto the front of the St. Andrews golfing society and, with a little stretching of the truth, the links were recognized as the official birthplace of golf. St. Andrews' terrain, its number of holes, the style of play it encouraged, became the standard of the sport. And, to this day, it is *the* definitive golf course.

So, whether a modern golfer plays alongside the beach in California, amidst cornfields in Kansas, in the suburbs of Tokyo, or high in the Himalayas, his game has been defined by Royal and Ancient Scottish standards established long ago.

At Braids Golf Course in Edinburgh (left) four lads discuss the game while a more seasoned player tees off at Turnberry Golf Course in Strathllyde (above). The Royal and Ancient Golf Club at St. Andrews in Fife (right) is the oldest golf course in the world and it was there that the eighteen hole course we know today was first designed.

The Lawn Tennis Championships

THE GAME MAY BE BASED ON THE medieval French *jeu de paume.* In recent years, it has been dominated by temperamental Yanks and masterful Swedes, Slavs, and Germans. But every summer, during the last week of June and the first week of July, an event takes place that transforms tennis into an indisputably British sport.

Locals, with typical understatement, refer to the event as "the Fortnight," because of its two-week duration. Officially, it's known as the Lawn Tennis Championships of the All-England Club. To the world at large, however, this blockbuster of tennis tournaments is known simply by the name of the London suburb in which it takes place: Wimbledon.

A tennis tournament has been played at Wimbledon annually (except during both world wars) since 1877, a scant four years after the modern game of lawn tennis was refined by a Briton, Major Walter Clopton Wingfield. He patented his lawn version of the sport, the game of tennis we know today, under the name of "sphairistike." Fortunately, the name didn't stick, but the game did.

The All-England Club itself was founded in 1868 for the playing of a less vigorous sport, croquet. But, its fortunes declining soon after its inception, the club built a few tennis courts in 1875 in the hope of attracting more members. The new game was such a success that within two years the All-England was holding its first championship tourney. Twenty-two aristocratic young men vied in the only competition held, the men's singles. The winner, Spencer Gore, a graduate of Harrow, defeated W. C. Marshall in three sets, 6–1, 6–2, 6–4, before a crowd of about two hundred.

Today, Wimbledon packs 10,651 seated and about 3,500 standing spectators into the twelve-sided stands surrounding the championship Centre Court. Thousands more cram in to view lesser stages of the men's and women's singles and doubles, and the mixed doubles, held either on the "number-one" court or one of the thirteen others set within the All-England Club's more than one thousand acres. Television coverage expands the audience even more, the viewership totaling in the hundreds of millions.

Despite the huge size of the present-day club, the media spectacle that the tournament has become, and the droves of foreigners who converge on both the stands and the grass courts, Wimbledon still manages to remain genteely English in

The Mansell Collection Ltd.

Wimbledon champions yesterday and today: William Renshaw defeats his twin brother Ernest Renshaw (left) in 1882 to win his second of six straight men's singles titles (Ernest won once in 1888, William a final time in 1889, and together they took men's doubles in 1880, 1881, 1884–1886, 1888, and 1889); Virginia Wade, who fell to Centre Court jitters in previous years (as in the match at right in 1975), went on to take the women's singles title in 1977.

Colorsport

character. The refreshment stands—both in the elite marquees of the Members' Enclosure and in the humbler precincts accommodating the ordinary fans—serve up strawberries at their sublime seasonal peak, with lashings of whipped cream. Fans queue politely for hours in the hope of getting a ticket to some match, any match; those with reserved seats who leave before a particular day's play ends generously oblige the waiting masses by leaving their tickets at the entrance gates for heavily discounted resale. And even the biggest brats of the tennis world seem better behaved, more gentlemanly, when they take to the Centre Court.

Tennis champions, whatever their country of origin, become *British*

champions on the Centre Court at Wimbledon. The enduring British love of fair play and a job well done causes Britons everywhere to take Wimbledon champions to their hearts, no matter how badly the local sporting press may have rebuked the same players' behavior earlier in the competition. Sadly, in recent years the British have *had* to adopt foreign Wimbledon champions as their own. Not since the great Fred Perry won the men's singles in 1934, 1935, and 1936 has a Briton dominated the sport, which made the Lawn Tennis Championships held in Wimbledon's Centenary Year of 1977—also the Silver Jubilee year of Queen Elizabeth II's reign—one of the most memorable in British sporting history.

In 1977 Virginia Wade was arguably Britain's finest female tennis player, though she had tried and failed in fifteen previous Wimbledons to win the championship. No one questioned her ability to be a champion (indeed, she had won the U.S. championship at Forest Hills in 1968), but she always seemed to falter when facing the pinnacle of British tennis. Not this time. Ginny, as she is called, beat the American Rosemary Casals in two sets in the quarterfinals. She smashed another American favorite, Chris Evert, 6–2, 4–6, 6–1 in the semifinals.

And then came the final match: Centre Court. For the first time since 1962, the Queen herself—no great lover of tennis—a vision in pink and

white, sat in the Royal Box. Ginny faced Betty Stove of the Netherlands, a mammoth woman of six-foot-one. Stove dominated Wade in the first set, winning six games to four. But Ginny, buoyed by the crowd's tremendous emotion and her own determination, came back to win the next two sets and the match, 6–3, 6–1.

It was a truly golden moment for British tennis, a classic example of the underdog turned proven champion. And the fans just had to show their profound sense of the occasion. Moments after the Queen had presented Virginia Wade with her trophy, with the cheers still echoing in Wimbledon's Centre Court, the crowd broke into a rousing chorus of "For She's a Jolly Good Fellow."

Rougher Sports: Soccer and Rugby

IN A NATION THAT USED TO PRIDE itself on being the most polite, civilized, and tolerant on earth, soccer, once Britain's sporting glory, is now often a shameful symbol of mindless modern violence. After the appalling scenes of rioting and death at the 1985 European Cup Final match between Liverpool and Juventus of Turin, Italy, British clubs were banned from foreign competition. For years, foreigners had put up with the drunken hooliganism of visiting British supporters, but in one horrifying night the time for decisive action finally had come.

Therefore, only the national teams of Great Britain are allowed to compete abroad, three of which—England, Scotland, and tiny Northern Ireland—qualified for the 1986 World Cup Finals in Mexico. The English haven't won the quadrennial World Cup competition since 1966, when they beat West Germany at Wembley Stadium in Northwest London. In recent years, the national teams have been eclipsed by the continental Europeans and the South Americans. But such local professional clubs as Liverpool, Everton, and Manchester United in England, and Celtic, Rangers, and Aberdeen in Scotland, still rank among the world's best—even if they aren't allowed to participate in international competitions.

At a domestic level, British soccer is primarily a gambling game. Every week during a season that now stretches from late August to May, millions of Brits dutifully fill in betting coupons, predicting the results of the Saturday league matches. The winners, sometimes of hundreds of thousands of pounds, are those who most accurately guess which matches will result in "score draws" —both teams scoring an equal number of goals. It's the nearest Britain comes to a national lottery.

First Division league games between the likes of Liverpool and Manchester United, Everton and Tottenham Hotspur, Arsenal and Nottingham Forest, attract twenty or thirty thousand spectators. In the lowly Fourth Division, the crowds are often measured in the hundreds. But even at the top end, facilities are often not up to professional, let alone safety, standards. Since a fire that destroyed the old wooden grandstand at Bradford and killed more than fifty supporters, the real deathtraps have been shut down. Still, despite the danger, large sections of soccer grounds consist of "terraces," in which the rule is "standing room only" where fans can crowd in to

Colorsport

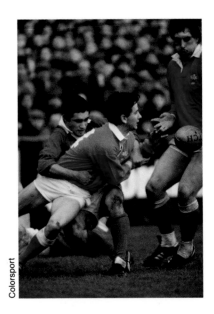

Colorsport

Colorsport

The rough and tumble action of rugby is clear in these photos (right and above) of the 1986 match between Wales and Ireland. In British soccer these days, there sometimes seems to be as much mayhem in the stands as on the field, leading some football grounds to erect strong barricades (left) to keep the fans where they belong.

watch the game, despite the danger.

Despite its decline, soccer is indisputably the major winter spectator sport. Right behind it comes rugby, the handling (as opposed to kicking) game played with an oval ball. It is divided into two different divisions—"League" (professional) and "Union" (amateur). Rugby League is essentially Northern and gritty, Union Southern and effete. At least that's the general image. The reality of it is more complex. In the coal mining towns of South Wales, for instance, Rugby Union is *the* game; every

miner plays it, and the rugby teams are incomparably more glamorous than the soccer teams.

Such complexities aside, one third of the English team that played against Ireland at Twickenham, Rugby Union's headquarters, in 1986 were recent graduates of Cambridge University. Rugby Union is as much a part of an English gentleman's education as the Church of England's "muscular Christianity." When sixty thousand or so spectators cram into Twickenham or the National Stadium at Cardiff, they invariably sing rude

songs and drink too much beer, just as well-brought-up young people ought to do. Sometimes an exhibitionist, male or female, may strip off and "streak" across the "pitch" (field), only to be carted off by the police, who use their helmets discreetly to shield the naughty bits. But, such high jinks aside, rugby fans don't beat people up, let alone stab them to death. You could take your dear old granny to a rugby match and not feel worried. Take her to a soccer match, however, and you might never see her again.

Chapter 12
Transportation

THERE ARE MANY LUXURY AUTO-mobiles manufactured throughout the world, and Britain produces its fair share, including the Aston Martin—made famous by Ian Fleming's fictional James Bond—the Bentley, and the Jaguar. But they all fade into the background when a Rolls-Royce motors into view. Of all luxury cars, only the Rolls was created not so much with a view toward luxury alone but out of a desire to produce the highest-quality automobile ever made.

By 1904, Frederick Henry Royce had already established himself as the designer and builder of three rudimentary but well-engineered two-cylinder motor cars. Charles Stewart Rolls was successfully selling automobiles to the gentry, but was frustrated by the lack of quality in the cars he sold. The two men met and formed a partnership in which Rolls had exclusive rights to sell automobiles designed by Royce. The car that resulted combined Royce's perfectionist engineering with Rolls's aristocratic appeal. It was a classic case of synergy: Rolls plus Royce equaled something many times greater than a simple sum of the two men's talents.

One of Rolls-Royce Ltd.'s first products proved the awesome power of the partnership. The car, introduced in 1907, was called the "40/50" (a measure of its horsepower). But

Automobiles of Luxury: Rolls-Royce

National Motor Museum, Beaulieu

The Rolls-Royce traditions of automotive craftsmanship and classic design are evident both in a 1907 40/50, better known as the "Silver Ghost" (left) and in a 1982 "Silver Spirit" (right). Since 1911, all Rolls-Royce motorcars have been graced with the company's hood ornament, "The Spirit of Ecstasy" (far right).

Rolls Royce Motor Cars Ltd.

National Motor Museum, Beaulieu

the shimmering aluminum paintwork and silver-plated accessories Rolls-Royce gave to a particular company show model won the entire line a more lasting sobriquet: the "Silver Ghost." To prove their car's superiority, Rolls-Royce sent the prototype Silver Ghost on a fifteen-thousand-mile test run, which it made without an involuntary stop—winning recognition as "The Best Car in the World." Over the next eighteen years, 7,800 Silver Ghosts were manufactured and sold.

Other classic models followed. In 1925, the company introduced the Phantom I, a car with a chassis similar to that of the Ghost but superior in performance, followed by the even more advanced Phantom II in 1929. Both models offered a variety of body choices: formal saloon cars, limousines, coupes, open touring cars, and so on. What they all had in common were Rolls-Royce's superior engineering and reliability. The company improved its engineering base even further with the acquisition in 1933 of the financially troubled Bentley company.

The years following World War II saw still more Rolls classics: the Silver Cloud series in 1955 (of which only 5,075 were produced), the Silver Shadow in 1965 (19,412 examples), and, more recently, the Silver Spirit, the Corniche, and the Camargue.

Though recent models definitely have a more modern look, they retain the roominess, comfort, quality, and air of noble dignity that Rolls-Royces have had from the start.

And there is, of course, the simple, unimpeachable luxury of the cars themselves. The flawless upholstery is made of the finest cow hides. The paneling comes from Circassian walnut trees, carefully cut into veneers that form perfectly symmetrical patterns and given a deep sheen with five coats of varnish. The Latin inscription that greets workers at Rolls-Royce's Crewe motor works—loosely translated as "Whatever is rightly done, however humble, is noble"—is

clearly no idle sentiment, it is a slogan for their standards of excellence.

There is one more element of the Rolls-Royce that has stayed constant virtually from the start. In 1911, the company introduced a silver winged female figure sculpted by Charles Sykes as a hood ornament. Known as "the Spirit of Ecstasy," it has become the symbol of the company and its fine automobiles. After the Ghost model, the figure was changed from a standing to a kneeling position, and modern safety regulations require that she retracts when the hood is accidentally bumped. But "Ecstasy" she remains, as stately as a Rolls-Royce automobile itself.

THE DEVELOPMENT OF HIGH-performance racing cars and sports cars calls for impeccably high standards of precision and quality, coupled with unswerving dedication and tenacity. No wonder, then, that British manufacturers have been at the forefront in the world of racing and sports cars ever since the invention of the automobile. Names like Sun-

Swallow Sidecar Company, which came to be known as makers of a "poor man's" answer to the Rolls-Royce. But after World War II, the name of one of Swallow's models became the name of the entire company, and few more fitting names could have been found for a manufacturer of sports cars: Jaguar. The company entered international racing

in 1949, and two years later a Jag won at Le Mans—the first British Grand Prix win since a Sunbeam victory thirty-two years earlier. Jaguar confirmed its growing reputation with three successive Le Mans wins in 1955, 1956, and 1957, all provided by its sleek D-type car. Since the 1960s, however, the company has concentrated on commercial produc-

Automobiles of Sport

beam, Aston Martin, Jaguar, MG, and Lotus are synonymous with speed and grace on the road.

In the years from 1908 to 1929, Sunbeam was the most successful racing car manufacturer in the world. Its cars held the world land speed record and were the first to exceed two hundred mph. Though British Sunbeams are no longer manufactured, (the name is now owned by the American Chrysler Corporation), they remain classic cars.

Aston Martin first made its name in 1908, when Lionel Martin proved his cars' extreme worthiness with a hill-climb victory at Aston Clinton. The company has since changed hands twice, and has been owned by Dave Brown since 1946; under his ownership, an Aston Martin won the prestigious French Grand Prix auto race at Le Mans in 1959. Today, Aston Martins tend more toward luxury than sport, with the comfortable four-seater Lagonda and the powerful DBS V8, but they still retain enough competitive spirit to shut down most challengers on the open road.

Few people have heard of the

National Motor Museum, Beaulieu

National Motor Museum, Beaulieu

tion, and its lasting contribution to the world of personal sports cars is the long, low, elegant E-type Jag.

The MG dominated the world of auto racing in the 1930s, a far cry from the humble automotive garage the company's founder William Morris opened in 1910. The MG-TC, introduced in 1948, was the first British sports car to overwhelmingly invade the United States. Relatively cheap, small, and light in weight, more than ten thousand were sold across the Atlantic in the first year alone, and the company enjoyed similar success with such models as the Austin-Healey Sprite, the MGA, and, for many the definitive sports car of the modern era, the MGB-GT. Sadly, financial problems have caused British Leyland, owners of MG in recent years, to close down the division.

The late Colin Chapman won the World Champion Car Constructor's prize more times than any other manufacturer with his highly successful Lotus sports car. Today, high performance Lotus road cars offer Porsche and Ferrari a run for their money, and the company's engineering knowledge is sought after and paid for handsomely by the world's major car manufacturers, among them Toyota and General Motors, guaranteeing the British sports car's rich past certain continuity into the future.

British sports cars have won international acclaim on both road and track. The 1958 Austin-Healy Sprite (left), manufactured by MG, was typical of the popular, inexpensive roadsters on which the company's success was built. The Jaguar E-type (right), commercial successor to the D-type that won at Le Mans, set new standards in sleek elegance. Cars from Lotus like the Esprit Turbo (above) offer championship design in a high-priced luxury road car.

National Motor Museum, Beaulieu

"WHAT IS THIS THAT ROARETH thus?" asked a very minor poet called A.D. Godley, who must have been a teacher of Latin:

Can it be a Motor Bus?
Yes, the smell and hideous hum
Indicat Motorem Bum!

is in traveling as well as arriving, you're much better off on a bus. Two of London's finest, most scenic journeys can be had by taking the 15, which runs through the City and Limehouse, or the 9, which takes in the western Thames on its route from Mortlake to Liverpool Street.

Upstairs on the bus affords the casual traveler a better view. But it is also the haven of smokers. If your lungs can't take it, travel by underground, where a total ban on smoking now exists.

"Underground" actually refers to the central parts of London's subway,

since the trains run above ground when they reach the suburbs. The Central Line goes right into rural Essex. The Metropolitan Line trundles way out into Buckinghamshire's Chiltern Hills. And there's quite a pretty stretch of District Line from Gunnersbury across the Thames at Strand-

The Bus and Underground

Nowadays, most people find the distinctive smell and hum (actually, more of a chortle than a hum) of a London bus rather cozy and reassuring. In a disconcerting modern world, the vivid scarlet double-decker bus is solidly old-fashioned. True, there have been modifications and some dreadful "refinements" (such as the abolition of strolling ticket collectors on certain routes); there are even some single-deckers operating in central London, such as the one that runs between Waterloo Station and Fleet Street. But in general the London bus is alive and well. It may sometimes be dirty, and more often never there when you want it, but it is nonetheless distinctively, perversely charming—as much a symbol of the city as Guardsmen in bearskin hats or Big Ben.

The consensus among London commuters is that the bus is less efficient but also less expensive and more fun than the "tube" or underground railway. Inefficiency is inevitable as long as London remains one of the world's great traffic jams, and it is only slightly relieved by the fact that there are now special bus lanes during rush hour. But if your interest

London Regional Transport

London Regional Transport

on-the-Green and on to Kew Gardens. In town, you have to content yourself with the brash new looks of such recently renovated stations as Baker Street, done up in a Sherlock Holmes motif, and Tottenham Court Road, with its colorful pop meanderings by artist Eduardo Paolozzi.

But the most colorful art of all connected with the tube is the London Underground Map, a miracle of clarity and one of the world's most popular pieces of graphic art. One authority suggests that the map must have been looked at "longer and with greater concentration than the *Night Watch*, the *Mona Lisa* and the *Laughing Cavalier* together." But, unlike those three great masterworks, the map remains a growing, changing, practical piece of art as London Transport continues to enlarge and improve its services.

London's buses and underground trains comprise one of the world's best public transportation systems. Night and day, double-deckers ply city and suburban streets (left). The complicated network of the Underground is more readily understood with this classic graphic design (right). London Transport has been modernizing stations throughout the city (above).

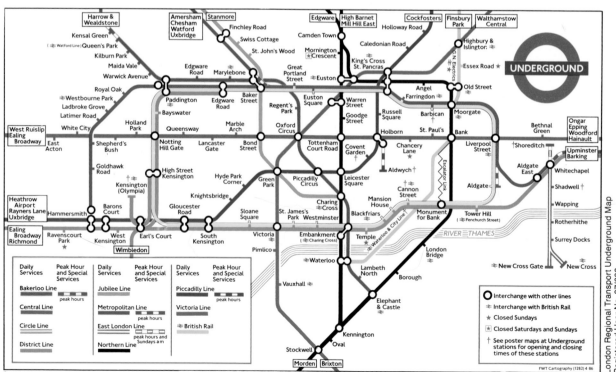

London Regional Transport Underground Map
Registered User No. 87/682

Chapter 13
On Holiday

Seaside Resorts

BIG, BRASH, AND JOVIAL, THE seaside resorts of Britain pull in native vacationers by the hundreds of thousands, often millions, each summer. In spite of the yearly exodus by package tourists to the predictably sizzling meccas of the Mediterranean, the majority of English, Welsh, and Scots head for the British seaside as soon as school "hols" and sunny bank holiday (i.e. three-day) weekends close in. If this leads to the customary logjams on the motorways (especially those radiating from London to the south coast), and the ensuing frayed nerves and tantrums, then the hope remains that it will all be worth the effort.

The largest of the British seaside resorts are great magnets that offer an inimitable mix of fun-fairs (carnivals), barrows (puchcarts) selling jellied eels and cockles, pubs, piers, and bandstands—an amalgam of old-fashioned and new-fangled diversions that appeals to both youngsters and adults. The names of the archetypal English resorts are known worldwide: Blackpool, Margate, Brighton, Torquay, Bournemouth, Great Yarmouth, and Sarborough. (Wales has its own crop of crowd-pullers in Colwyn Bay, Rhyl, and Llandudno, while Scottish resorts rely on the more sedate pleasures of fine beaches and unspoiled countryside rather than flash and fun.)

If visitors cannot always be assured of sun (reliable English summers being as rare as hen's teeth), they can at least find miles of sand at the big resorts, along with an unparalleled array of entertainments: miniature train rides, aquariums, boating lakes, amusement arcades alive with video games and slot machines (called locally "fruit" machines, after the winning combinations of cherries, oranges, lemons, and so on), summer shows, discos, heated swimming pools, and rickety roller coasters. Blackpool's famed Pleasure Beach Amusement Park alone covers some forty acres.

Seafront souvenir shops sell an eyepopping array of seaside kitsch

BTA

Britain's seaside resorts tempt vacationers with pleasures both homespun and sensual. Long stretches of beach like the one at Eastbourne (left) beckon sun worshippers to pull up a gaily striped deck chair, while more active holiday-makers can explore the attractions on the pier. At Brighton, there's the famous Pavilion (right) to visit. And anyone can send a saucy seaside postcard (far right) to those less fortunate folks back home.

and paraphernalia that has seduced generations of children and their parents. You can spend your holiday pounds on water-wings, buckets and spades, sunhats emblazoned with "Kiss Me Quick," pink or multicolored sticks of "rock"—hard candy shaped like a barber's pole, with the resort's name ingeniously written through its center, like a ring in a tree trunk—and those wonderful comic postcards of ludicrously large wives, weedy husbands, and saucy *double entendres* beloved by the crowds since Victorian times.

Down on the beach, the adults sunbathe or sit in deckchairs wrapped up against a chill wind.

Meanwhile, children build sandcastles, go for donkey rides, scour rock pools for shrimp, or watch Punch and Judy, a traditional puppet show that still enthralls the young with its knockabout comedy and stock figures of fun.

England has more than ninety seaside resorts, each with its own special character. Queen of the south coast is Brighton. A fishing village in the mid-eighteenth century, it leaped to popularity after a Sussex doctor proclaimed the health benefits of sea air and salt-water bathing. The arrival of the Prince Regent, and his construction there of the exotic personal pleasure palace known as the Royal

Pavilion, ensured the town's fashionability. Today, Brighton's elegant Regency buildings are considered one of the glories of English architecture.

Blackpool, in Lancashire on England's northwest coast, draws six to eight million visitors each year. Its countless attractions include a seven-mile seafront served by electric trams and illuminated every autumn with brilliant lighting tableaux. Of equal fame to "the Lights" is the 518-foot-tall Blackpool Tower, whose bowels contain, among other things, a circus and a splendid ballroom where couples can waltz to the resounding chords of a mighty Wurlitzer organ.

What symbolizes for many the es-

sence of the seaside holiday at any British resort is the pier—that great promenade stretching out into the sea, from whose deck rises a magical concoction of fun palaces, theaters, pavilions, and wind breaks, all topped with Oriental domes and turrets and strung with twinkling fairy lights. At the height of the Victorian era, there were a hundred such piers, though storms, fire, and decay have reduced that number by half. Whether seen at their bustling best in July and August, or dismal and windswept in winter (a distinct preference with more melancholic Britons), the pier will always capture the true spirit of the British seaside holiday.

Country Rambles

THE BEST WAY TO DISCOVER BRITain is on foot or on horseback. Leaving the main road, you leave the twentieth century behind and experience a rural land largely unspoiled by the noise, pollution, and urban eyesores of modern life.

No wonder, then, that so many Britons choose country rambles as their holiday getaways. Indeed, it has been estimated that one in five Britons takes a walk of several miles at least once each week. The British still believe soundly in the benefits of good, clean, bracing air, beautiful scenery, and a touch of physical exertion to cure whatever ails you. Whenever weather allows (and frequently when those of less robust and diffident nationalities would figure the weather doesn't allow), you'll see them striding out through the alpine meadows of the Lake District; among the rolling hills of the Cotswolds; across the broad expanses of the Yorkshire Moors or the Scottish Highlands; along the ancient earthwork of Offa's Dyke on the English–Welsh border; or anywhere else that Britain's diverse landscape offers a navigable path and a pleasing view.

Connoisseurs of country walking know that each path holds its own distinctive pleasures. In the Lake District, one could easily succumb to the illusion that it really was Switzerland (indeed, the area convincingly doubled for the Alps in several scenes of British director Ken Russell's film *Mahler*). There, too, one can delve into the lives of England's "Lake Poets," particularly William Wordsworth, whose homes can be visited in and around Grasmere. In the Cotswolds, there's the pleasure of

seeing the appropriately named Cotswold stone, a local pale-colored limestone that is used in all the buildings in the region, giving small towns, cottages, barns, and businesses a gentle visual unity that melds beautifully with the green countryside.

The Scottish Highlands offer high drama: a walk along the banks of Loch Lomond on a stormy day, for example, its romantic vista punctuated with not one, not two, but *seven* overlapping rainbows. Offa's Dyke continually exposes the rambler to the drama of British history, as one passes the ruins of ancient priories set in wild landscapes perfect for

BTA

Whether on foot or by pony, trekking is a favored pastime of Britons. In Cumbria, in England's Lake District (left), hikers are bound to discover an endless array of spectacular mountainous skylines, while the Cornish Coastal Footpath (below) offers the craggy coastline for which England is famous. The Black Mountains in the county of Powys in Wales (far left) offer more challenging terrain that is ideal for pony-trekking.

meditation and massive castles that harken back to the days when England and Wales were not united under a common banner. And all routes offer the delights of discovering country inns and pubs.

For those vacationers who want the scenery and the sense of rural isolation without quite so much physical exertion, many parts of Britain today are settings for pony-trekking—particularly remote parts of Wales and Scotland. Settled down comfortably on the back of a gentle, slow-moving and sure-footed Welsh cob, Welsh pony, or Highland pony, riders are led by a guide cross-country through truly spectacular landscapes. Beginning pony-trekkers often stay at a pony trekking center, from which they ride forth each morning on a carefully selected route. The more advanced, however, participate in "post trekking," following centuries-old routes and stopping each night at a different country hotel, hostel, or farmhouse.

Comfortably bedded down, with the only sounds being, perhaps, the stirring of the ponies outside, it is easy to forget the modern world and to feel oneself a part of the countryside—something very old and basic, something essentially British.

FOR A CENTURY AND A HALF, LUX-urious travel has been virtually synonymous with the name of one company in Britain: Cunard. Since the line's first vessel, a small 1,154-ton wooden paddlewheeler named *Britta-nia,* made its maiden crossing of the Atlantic in 1840, Cunard has de-

Cunard's line of luxury ships provided more than fun enough. Their names today read like a litany of sea-going legends: *Aquitania, Lusitania, Mauretania, Queen Mary, Queen Eliz-abeth,* and *Queen Elizabeth II* (known affectionately as the *QE2*).

These splendid floating grand ho-

class cabins were the epitome of indulgence, outfitted in the latest style of furnishings, comfortable sitting rooms, lavish private baths, and even separate, rather more spartan, quarters for one's maid or manservant.

Add to such features, of course, the most proper elements of British

And their effect was not lost on even the most famous and worldly of passengers. "If there ever was a ship which possessed a thing called 'soul,' the *Mauretania* does," wrote President Franklin Delano Roosevelt after a trans-Atlantic passage aboard her. "Every ship has a soul, but the *Mauretania* had one you could talk to. At times she would be wayward and contrary as a thoroughbred. As the captain once said to me, she had the manners and deportment of a great lady and behaved herself as such."

"Half the Fun"

fined—to the most discriminating of British standards—the concept of traveling in style.

Indeed, the company's famous advertising slogan has become a catchphrase of sophisticated travelers. "Getting there is half the fun," its posters and ads proclaimed, and

tels set the highest of standards. Their public rooms were decorated with marble, gilt, wood paneling, velvet drapes, crystal, and mirrors. Original oil paintings graced their walls (or, more strictly speaking, their bulkheads), full-grown trees and antique furniture their passageways. First-

decorum. High tea was offered daily in the ship's dining rooms. If the air out on deck had a bit of a nip to it, a steward was always on hand to drape one with an afghan "rug." Such touches gave a decidedly homey, personal air to what might otherwise have seemed imposing surroundings.

But we live now in another time and another world. It's a world in which manners and deportment don't seem to matter as much; in which the fuel costs of driving the turbines to power a vessel weighing tens of thousands of tons push fares

Courtesy of Cunard

The only ship to make regular Transatlantic crossings, Cunard's QE2 (left and right) is one of the last great ocean liners still voyaging to Europe in style. In the tradition of her predecessors, the original Queen Elizabeth *and the* Queen Mary, *the QE2 boasts a number of dining rooms, ball rooms, a casino, theaters, swimming pools, and more to keep her passengers resting happily in the lap of luxury.*

Roger Hutchings/Network

prohibitively high; in which people are too rushed to spend several days at sea when they can make the same journey in several hours; in which few people seem to care any more about the fun of getting there.

Of the soulful *Mauretania* and its sister ships in the Cunard Line, only the *QE2* sails the seas today, carrying passengers across the Atlantic and on Caribbean and round-the-world cruises. It *is*, to be sure, a marvelous vessel, weighing in at 67,107 tons, with four swimming pools (two indoors, two out), thirty public rooms, four dining rooms, six cocktail lounges, a shopping arcade, beauty salon and barber shop, saunas and Turkish baths, two libraries, a casino, kennels, complete medical and dental clinics, a computer room (for onboard hacks), four orchestras, nightly double-bill first-run movies, and on, and on, and on.

Yet one cannot help but mourn the passing of her sisters. And none more plaintively than the proud *Queen Mary.* Cunard put her out of service in 1967, and sold her—no doubt to the shock of her passenger-alumni and crew—to the city of Long Beach, just south of Los Angeles. There she sits today, locked in concrete on the edge of a harbor where pleasure craft and sailboaters go whizzing by. She's now a tourist attraction, surrounded by a "British" village of shops so saccharine in its conception and execution that it would set even Walt Disney's teeth on edge. American daytrippers and tourists from all over the world can roam the great lady's decks at their pleasure, viewing what luxury life afloat must have been like—yet never really getting to *experience* it. All the pleasure of being there is, sadly, now gone.

Sources

Canada

Antiques

Deeler's Antiques
3055 South Granville Street
Vancouver, British Columbia
V6H 3K1
(604) 738-2223

Sotheby Parke Bernet & Co.
9 Hazelton Avenue
Toronto, Ontario
M5R 2E1
(416) 926-1774

Books, Periodicals, and Records

Collectors RPM
456 Seymour Street
Vancouver, British Columbia
V6B 3H1
(604) 685-8841
British imports and Beatles museum

European News Import House
1136 Robson Street
Vancouver, British Columbia
V6E 1B2
(604) 683-0616

Gordon & Gotch Canada Ltd.
55 York Street
Toronto, Ontario
M5J 1S4
(416) 586-0500

Odyssey Imports
866 Granville Street
Vancouver, British Columbia
V6B 3J5
(604) 669-6644
British import records

Siana Flewog
Jane Hughes
329 Queenston Street
St. Catherines, Ontario
L2P 2X8
(416) 684-5913
Welsh books, music, and folk art

W.H. Smith
113 Merton Street
Toronto, Ontario
M4S 1A8
(416) 485-6660

650 W. Georgia Street
Vancouver Centre
Vancouver, British Columbia
V6V 4N7
(604) 689-5323

Fashions

General

Aquascutum Canada Ltd.
2520 St. Josephs Boulevard East
Montréal, Québec
H1Y 2A2
(514) 527-9321

Holt Renfrew & Co.
50 Bloor Street West
Toronto, Ontario
M4W 1A1
(416) 922-2333

Jaeger
The Colonnade
131 Bloor Street West
Toronto, Ontario
M5S 1R1
(416) 966-3544

Jaegar at the Bay
200 Eighth Avenue SW
Calgary, Alberta
T2P 1B5
(403) 233-8573

Jaeger International Shop
2450 Boulevard Laurirer
Place St. Foy, Québec
G1V 2L1
(418) 653-0993

Marks & Spencer
3770 Nashua Drive
Mississauga, Ontario
L4V 1M6
(416) 676-1910

556 Granville Street
Vancouver, British Columbia
V6C 1W6
(604) 685-8481

Ogilvy's
1307 St. Catherine Street West
Montréal, Québec
H3G 1P7
(514) 842-7711
Traditional Scottish goods

Simpson's
977 St. Catherine Street West
Montréal, Québec
H3B 3Y7
(514) 284-4231

401 Bay Street
Toronto, Ontario
M5H 2Y4
(416) 861-9111

Men's

Eaton's
1 Dundas Street West
Toronto, Ontario
M5B 1CB
(416) 343-2111

Edward Chapman
833 West Pender Street
Vancouver, British Columbia
V6C 1K7
(604) 685-6207

Women's

Laura Ashley
1171 Robson Street
Vancouver, British Columbia
V6E 1B1
(604) 688-8729

18 Hazelton Avenue
Toronto, Ontario
M5R 2E2
(416) 922-7761

2110 Crescent Street
Montréal, Québec
H3G 2B8
(514) 284-9225

Government Offices

British Consulate-General
Suite 1404
10025 Jasper Avenue
Edmonton, Alberta
T5J 1S6
(403) 428-0375

Suite 800
1111 Melville Street
Vancouver, British Columbia
V6E 3V6
(604) 683-4421

Suite 1910
College Park
777 Bay Street
Toronto, Ontario
M5G 2G2
(416) 593-1290

Room 901
635 Dorchester Boulevard West
Montréal, Québec
H35 1R6
(514) 866-5863

British High Commission
80 Elgin Street
Ottawa, Ontario
K1P 5K7
(613) 237-1530

Organizations

British Canadian Trade Association (BCTA)
7100 Woodbine Avenue
Suite 106
Markham, Ontario
L3R 5J2
(416) 475-3896

Clans & Scottish Societies of Canada
95 Laurel Avenue
Islington, Ontario
M9B 4T1
(416) 593-4095

English-Speaking Union
P.O. Box 308
Ottawa, Ontario
K1N 8V3
(613) 733-0296

40 St. Clair Avenue East
Toronto, Ontario
M4T 1M9
(416) 925-7860

1260 University Street
Suite 201
Montréal, Québec
H3B 3B9
(514) 861-8186

Ontario Gymanfa Ganu Association
20 Deerfield Drive
Suite 1605
Napean, Ontario
K76 4L2
Welsh organization

St. Andrew's Society
122 Westmount Avenue
Toronto, Ontario
M6H 3K4

St. Ann's Gaelic College
Baddeck
Cape Breton, Nova Scotia

St. David's Society
33 Melrose Avenue
Toronto, Ontario
M5M 1Y6

St. George's Society
14 Elm Street
Toronto, Ontario
M5G 1G7
(416) 597-0220

Scottish Heritage Society of Canada
P.O. Box 38
Tower Royal Bank
Toronto, Ontario
M5J 2J7

Pottery and Porcelain

Ashley China
50 Bloor Street West
Toronto, Ontario
M4W 3L8
(416) 964-2900

Bradshaw's China Hall
129 Ontario Street
Stratford, Ontario
N5A 6T7
(519) 271-6283

Caplan Duval
6700 Cote des Neiges
Montréal, Québec
H3S 2B2
(514) 483-4040

The Glass House
503 Portage Avenue
Winnipeg, Manitoba
R3B 2E3
(204) 775-0439

Lawleys of London
Sunridge Mall
2525 36th Street NE
Calgary, Alberta
T1Y 5T4
(403) 285-5529

McIntosh & Watts
2425 Holly Lane
Ottawa, Ontario
K1V 5B9
(613) 523-7120

Mary's China Shop
3310 Dougall Avenue
Windsor, Ontario
N9E 1S8
(519) 258-4131

Murchie's Tea & Coffee Ltd.
1200 Homer Street
Vancouver, British Columbia
V6B 2Y5
(604) 662-3776

Piccadilly
2102 11th Avenue
Cornwell Mall
Regina, Saskatchewan
S4P 2B6
(306) 522-6940

The Registry
2672 West Edmonton Mall
8770 170th Street
Edmonton, Alberta
T5T 4J2
(403) 487-6683

Royal Worcester Spode
35 Prince Andrew Place
Don Mills, Ontario
M3C 2H2
(416) 445-2225

Wedgwood (Canada) Ltd.
271 Yorkland Boulevard
Willowdale, Ontario
M2J 1S6
(416) 491-9630

Publications

Britannia
117 Queen Street E
Toronto, Ontario
M5C 1S2
(416) 361-3400

The Scottish Banner
Box 200
Station H
Toronto, Ontario
M4C 5J2
(416) 751-6000

Sports

Antigonish Highland Games
Antigonish Highland Society
274 Main Street
Antigonish, Nova Scotia
B2G 2C4
Annual Scottish games in mid-July

Royal Canadian Henley Regatta
St. Catharines, Ontario
Annual regatta in August

Theater

The Shaw Festival
P.O. Box 774
Niagara-on-the-Lake, Ontario
L0S 1J0
(416) 468-2172

Stratford Shakespearean Festival
P.O. Box 520
Stratford, Ontario
N5A 6V2
(519) 271-4040

Travel

British Airways
1176 West Georgia Street
Suite 1200
Vancouver, British Columbia
V6E 2Y2
(604) 222-2508

1021 Boulevard de Maison Neuve Ouest
Montréal, Québec
H3A 2C8
(514) 287-9282

British Caledonian Airways
Suite 1502
Royal Trust Tower
P.O. Box 355
Toronto Dominion Centre
Toronto, Ontario
M5K 1K7
(800) 344-BCAL

British Rail
409 Granville Street
Vancouver, British Columbia
V6C 1T2
(604) 683-6896

94 Cumberland Street
Toronto, Ontario
M5R 1A3
(416) 929-3333

British Tourist Authority
409 Granville Street
Suite 451
Vancouver, British Columbia
V6C 1T2
(604) 669-2414

94 Cumberland Street
Suite 600
Toronto, Ontario
M5R 1A3
(416) 925-6326

United States

Antiques

Christie, Manson & Woods International, Inc.
502 Park Avenue
New York, NY 10022
(212) 546-1000

Christie's East
219 East 67th Street
New York, NY 10021
(212) 606-0400

Old World Antiques
8226 West 3rd Street
Los Angeles, CA 90048
(213) 653-1400

Sotheby Park Bernet Inc.
308 North Rodeo Drive
Beverly Hills, CA 90210
(213) 274-0340

1334 York Avenue
New York, NY 10021
(212) 606-7000

Stair & Company Inc.
58 East 57th Street
New York, NY 10022
(212) 517-4400

Stair's Incurable Collector
42 East 57th Street
New York, NY 10022
(212) 755-0140

Sylvia Tearston
1053 Third Avenue
New York, NY 10021
(212) 838-0415

Trevor Potts Antiques
1011 Lexington Avenue
New York, NY 10021
(212) 737-0909

Welsh Heritage Antiques
108 Clover Lane
Mankato, MN 56001
(507) 726-6162

Automobile Clubs

American MGB Association
Box 11401-R
Chicago, IL 60611
(312) 843-3897

Austin-Healey Club of America
603 East Euclid Avenue
Arlington Heights, IL 60004

Lotus Ltd.
Box L
College Park, MD 20740

TR3 Car Club of America
5112 Wapakoneta Road
Bethesda, MD 20816

Vintage Triumph Register
Box 36477
Grosse Pointe, MI 48236

Books and Records

Anne Habermehl Welsh Imports
3925 North Main Street
Marion, NY 14505
(315) 926-5318

Book and Record Mart
44 South Main Street
Wilkes-Barre, PA 18701
(717) 825-4767

British Gifts
Box 26558
Los Angeles, CA 90026

British Market Inc.
2366 Rice Boulevard
Houston, TX 77005
(713) 529-9889

British Travel Bookshop
40 West 57th Street
New York, NY 10019
(212) 765-0898

Celtic Books & Media
P.O. Box 2388
Dublin, CA 94568

East of Hebrides
507 Germantown Pike
Lafayette Hill, PA 19444
(215) 825-7268

GHS Inc/British Travel Bookshop
Box 1224
Clifton, NJ 07012
(212) 765-0898

House of Books
1758 Gardenaire Lane
Anaheim, CA 92804
Scottish & Welsh books

Murder Ink
271 West 87th Street
New York, NY 10024
(212) 362-8905
Detective fiction

The Rivendell Book Shop
109 St. Mark's Place
New York, NY 10009
(212) 533-2501

The Welsh Dragon
211 Main Street
Annapolis, MD 21401
(301) 267-8491

Collectibles and Crafts

British Regalia Imports
P.O. Box 50473
Nashville, Tennessee 37205
Militaria

Celtic Photos & Crafts
10 Hemingway Road
North Haven, CT 06473

The Crafty Scot
P.O. Box 5043
Greenville, SC 29606
Scottish cross-stitching kits

The Gaelic Shop
P.O. Box 6
New Hope, PA 18938
(215) 862-9285
Tartan blankets and other items

Holloway House
126 East Main Street
Lititz, PA 17543
Royal collectibles

London Antiques
930 E. Street
San Diego, CA 92101
(800) 223-8579/325-4489

McMamara's Green
P.O. Box 1111
Salem, OR 97308
(503) 581-1237

Scotsworld Ltd.
P.O. Box 434
Fairfax Station, VA 22039
(800) 423-6556

Tartans Unlimited
Box 33822
San Diego, CA 92103
Scottish militaria

The Welsh and American Sewing Company
1701 Ocean Drive
Oxnard, CA 93035
Needlework kits

Fashions
General

Aquascutum of London
680 Fifth Avenue
New York, NY 10019
(212) 975-0250

Aquascutum Palm Beach
237A Worth Avenue
Palm Beach, FL 33480
(305) 833-3808

Barney's
106 7th Avenue
New York, NY 10011
(212) 929-9000

Bigsby & Kruthers
1750 North Clark Street
Chicago, IL 60614
Aquascutum
(312) 440-1750

Burberrys Ltd.
9 East 57th Street
New York, NY 10022
(212) 371-5010

633 North Michigan Avenue
Chicago, IL 60611
(312) 787-2500

1705 Walnut Street
Philadelphia, PA 19103
(215) 557-7400

1155 Connecticut Avenue
Washington, DC 20036
(202) 463-3000

David Morgan
11812 Northcreek Parkway N.
Suite 103
Bothell, WA 98011
(206) 485-2132
Welsh woolens

Geoffrey (Tailor) Highland Crafts of USA Inc.
384 Oyster Point Boulevard #7
South San Francisco, CA 94080
(415) 583-3175
Traditional Scottish Highland dress

The Great Scot Trading Co.
P.O. Box 1744
New Orleans, LA 70004
(504) 831-8638
Kilts

Higbees Department Store
26500 Cedar Road
Beechwood, OH 44122
(216) 464-6000

100 Public Square
Cleveland, OH 44113
(216) 579-2580

Jaeger International Shop
9699 Wilshire Boulevard
Beverly Hills, CA 90212
(213) 276-1062

272 Post Street
San Francisco, CA 94108
(415) 421-3714

835 North Michigan Avenue
Chicago, IL 60611
(312) 642-6665

Copley Place
100 Huntington Avenue
Boston, MA 02116
(617) 437-1163

818 Madison Avenue
New York, NY 10021
(212) 638-3350

1719 Walnut Street
Philadelphia, PA 19103
(215) 751-9285

Charleston Place
130 Market Street
Charleston, SC 29401

Raleighs
1201 Connecticut Avenue
Washington, DC 20036
(202) 785-7071

Saks Fifth Avenue
Post & Powell Streets
San Francisco, CA 94108
(415) 986-4300

Tartan Imports of Florida
1507 Main Street
Dunedin, FL 33528
(813) 736-2006
Complete Highland dress

Men's

Ben Silver
149 King Street
Charleston, SC 29401
(803) 577-4556

Clacton and Frinton
731 North La Cienaga Boulevard
West Hollywood, CA 90069
(213) 652-2957

Kent & Curwen
474 North Rodeo Drive
Beverly Hills, CA 90210
(213) 274-0233

Rosenthal-Truitt
Sunset Plaza
8648 Sunset Boulevard
Los Angeles, CA 90069
(213) 659-5470

Women's

Laura Ashley
121 North La Cienaga Boulevard
Los Angeles, CA 90048
(213) 854-0490

1827 Union Street
San Francisco, CA 94102
(415) 788-0190

3213 M Street, NW
Washington, DC 20007
(202) 338-5481

320 Worth Avenue
Palm Beach, FL 33480
(305) 832-3188

Watertower Place
Chicago, IL 60611
(312) 951-8004

21 East 57th Street
New York, NY 10022
(212) 735-1010

Galleria
Dallas, TX 75240
(214) 980-9858

405 University Street
Seattle, WA 98101
(206) 343-9637

Edina and Lena
9528 Santa Monica Boulevard
Beverly Hills, CA 90210
(213) 275-6869
Handknits

Victoria Falls
147 Spring Street
New York, NY 10012
(212) 226-5099
Antique Victorian

Furnishings and Interior Design

The Artful Dodger's Pine Mine
7974 Melrose Avenue
West Hollywood, CA 90069
(213) 653-9726
English country pine

Bac St. Antiques
8428 Melrose Place
West Hollywood, CA 90069
(213) 653-3899

Conran's
Chapel Square Mall
900 Chapel Street
New Haven, CT 06510
(203) 782-1612

Georgetown Park
3227 Grace Street NW
Washington, DC 20007
(202) 298-8300

26 Exeter Street
Boston MA 02116
(617) 266-2836

The Market at Citicorp
160 East 54th Street
New York, NY 10022
(212) 371-2225

The Plaza at King of Prussia
160 North Gulph Road
King of Prussia, PA 19406
(215) 337-8322

Conran's Mail Order
4 South Middlesex Avenue
Cranbury, NJ 08512
(609) 655-4505

Hunt Galleries, Inc.
P.O. Box 2324
Hickory, NC 28603
(704) 324-9934
English country-style

James M. Hansen
27 East De La Guerra Street
Santa Barbara, CA 93101
(805) 963-6827

Magnolia Hall
726 Andover
Atlanta, GA 30327
Antique replicas

Martha M. House
1022 South Decatur Street
Montgomery, AL 36104
(205) 264-3558
Victorian-style

Raintree Designs
D&D Building
979 Third Avenue
New York, NY 10022
(212) 477-8591
English country decoration

Gardens

Huntington Botanical Gardens
1151 Oxford Road
San Marino, CA 91108
Shakespeare garden

Mohonk Mountain House Gardens
Mohonk Lake
New Paltz, NY 12561
Victorian garden

Morris Arboretum
University of Pennsylvania
9414 Meadowbrook Avenue
Philadelphia, PA 19118
English landscape style

Old Westbury Gardens
P.O. Box 420
Old Westbury, NY 11568
Late 19th-century Victorian

Tryon Palace Restoration
613 Pollack Street
New Bern, NC 28560
English landscape style

Woodlawn Plantation
Mount Vernon, VA 22121
Naturalistic English-style

Government Offices

British Consulate
10th Floor
321 St. Charles Avenue
New Orleans, LA 70130
(504) 586-1979

813 Stemmons Tower West
2730 Stemmons Freeway
Dallas, TX 75207
(214) 637-3600

British Consulate-General
3701 Wilshire Boulevard
Los Angeles, CA 90010
(213) 385-7381

33 North Dearborn Street
Chicago, IL 60602
(312) 346-1810

4740 Prudential Tower
Boston, MA 02199
(617) 437-7160

845 Third Avenue
New York, NY 10022
(212) 752-8400

1650 The Illuminating Building
55 Public Square
Cleveland, OH 44113
(216) 621-7674

Suite 2250, Dresser Tower
601 Jefferson
Houston, TX 77002
(713) 659-6270

British Embassy
3100 Massachusetts Avenue, NW
Washington, DC 20008
(202) 462-1340

Music

American Friends of Scottish Opera, Inc.
281 Park Avenue South
5th Floor
New York, NY 10010
(212) 674-7491

Grenadier Music
P.O. Box 1128
Seneca, SC 29678
Celtic harps & folk instruments

Lyon & Healy
168 North Ogden Avenue
Chicago, IL 60607
(312) 786-1881
(800) 621-3881
Makers of Welsh folk harps

Ninnau Welsh Talent Agency
10 Hemingway Road
North Haven, CT 06473
(203) 239-1410
Books the Orpheus Male Voice Choir, among others

Organizations

American Scottish Foundation, Inc.
P.O. Box 537 Lenox Hill Station
New York, NY 10021
(212) 988-4468

British-American Chamber of Commerce
275 Madison Avenue
New York, NY 10016
(212) 889-0680

British & Commonwealth Institute of New York
60 East 42nd Street,
Suite 2140
New York, NY 10165

The British Club of Chicago
2357 West Chase Avenue
Chicago, IL 60645
(312) 465-9405

British Information Services
845 Third Avenue
New York, NY 10022
(212) 752-8400

Council of British Societies
P.O. Box 49804
Los Angeles, CA 90049
(213) 826-4985

Council of Scottish Clan Associations Inc.
929 Cooper Avenue
Columbus, GA 31906

Cuideagh O C'orn O Uisghebeathe
(Society of Tasters of Whisky)
4356 Lynnville Crescent
Virginia Beach, VA 23452
(804) 340-2721

English-Speaking Union
253 South Oxford Avenue
Los Angeles, CA 90004
(213) 383-8051

  Metropolitan Club
  640 Sutter Street
  San Francisco, CA 94102
  (415) 673-7313

  2131 S Street, NW
  Washington, DC 20008
  (202) 234-4602

  612 North Michigan Avenue, #513
  Chicago, IL 60611
  (312) 642-1020

  44 Commonwealth Avenue
  Boston, MA 02116
  (617) 536-4740

  16 East 69th Street
  New York, NY 10021
  (212) 879-6800

  251 South 18th Street
  Philadelphia, PA 19103
  (215) 545-3619

  2600 Southwest Freeway
  Houston, TX 77098
  (713) 524-1341

International Society for British Genealogy and
  Family History
P.O. Box 220425
Cleveland, OH 44120

National Welsh-American Foundation
P.O. Box 297
Pottsville, PA 17901

The Royal Oak Foundation, Inc.
41 East 72nd Street
New York, NY 10021
(212) 861-0529
*Affiliated with the National Trust of England,
Wales, and Northern Ireland*

St. Andrew's Society of Detroit
St. Andrew's Hall
431 East Congress Street
Detroit, MI 48226

St. Andrew's Society of San Francisco
333 Kearny Street #210
San Francisco, CA 94108

St. Andrew's Society of the State of New York
281 Park Avenue South
New York, NY 10010
Scottish organization

St. David's Society of the State of New York
71 West 23rd Street
New York, NY 10010
(212) 924-8415
Welsh organization

Scottish-American Society of Central Florida
P.O. Box 2149
Orlando, FL 32802

Scottish American Society of South Florida
P.O. Box 633
Miami Shores, FL 33153

The Scottish Cultural Society, Ltd.
2801 North Elmwood
Waukegan, IL 60087

Scottish Development Agency
1 Landmark Square
Suite 810
Stamford, CT 06901

Scottish Heritage USA Inc.
281 Park Avenue South
5th Floor
New York, NY 10010
(212) 674-7491

Texas Scottish Clan Gathering Association
4302 Airport Blvd.
Austin, TX 78722

United Scottish Society Inc.
7415 Faust Avenue
Canoga Park, CA 91307
(818) 703-0341

Welsh Associated Youth
c/o Jay G. Williams III
300 College Hill Road
Clinton, NY 13323

Welsh National Gymanfa Ganu Association,
  Inc.
c/o Mrs. Nancy Miller
95 Concord Road
Acton, MA 01720

Pottery and Porcelain

The China Warehouse
Box 21797
Cleveland, OH 44121
(216) 831-2557
(800) 321-3212

Geary's
351 N. Beverly Drive
Beverly Hills, CA 90210
(213) 272-9334

R.B. Heslop
22790 Heslop Drive
Novi, MI 48050
(800) 538-6340

James Kaplan Jewelers
Garden City Shopping Center
Cranston, RI 02920
(800) 343-0712

Tilden Thurber
292 Westminster Mall
Providence, RI 02903
(800) 848-7237

Wedgwood
304 Stockton Street
San Francisco, CA 94108
(415) 391-5610

  The Galleria
  5085 Westheimer
  Suite 3745
  Houston, TX 77056
  (713) 627-0642

  636 North Michigan Avenue
  Chicago, IL 60611
  (312) 944-1994/1995

Publications

The British Observer
2269 Market Street #136
San Francisco, CA 94114
(415) 864-3349

British Weekly
1936 14th Street
Santa Monica, CA 90404
(213) 450-3711

Illustrated London News
c/o British Publications Inc.
11-03 46th Avenue
Long Island City, NY 11101

IN BRITAIN
Box 1238
Allwood
Clifton, NJ 07012

NINNAU
The North American Welsh Newspaper
11 Post Terrace
Basking Ridge, NJ 07920
(201) 766-6736

Royal Book News
c/o Marlene Eilers
11 Hester Street
Little Ferry, NJ 07643
Newsletter about books on royalty

The Scottish-American
P.O. Box 4473
Star City, WV 26505
(304) 599-1877

True Brit
P.O. Box 4475
Chatsworth, CA 91313
(818) 998-0511

U.K. Magazine
P.O. Box 25
Hatboro, PA 19040

Union Jack
P.O. Box 1823
La Mesa, CA 92041
(619) 466-3129

Sports

Action Youth/International Sports Council
P.O. Box 3071
Long Beach, CA 90803
(213) 434-6741
(800) 523-1741
Organizes soccer tours to Britain

New Hampshire Highland Games
P.O. Box 130
Cambridge, MA 02238
(617) 864-8945

Ohio Scottish Games, Inc.
P.O. Box 21169
Cleveland, OH 44121

Stone Mountain Highland Games Inc.
Box 14023
Atlanta, GA 30324
(404) 396-5728

United States Polo Association
1301 West 22nd Street
Oak Brook, IL 60521
(312) 654-1631

Theater

American Friends of the Royal Shakespeare
    Theatre, Inc.
c/o Wintrop, Stimson, Putnam and Roberts
40 Wall Street
New York, NY 10005
(212) 943-0700

Shakespeare

Adams Memorial Theatre
Southern Utah State College
Cedar City, UT 84720
(801) 586-7878

The Folger Shakespeare Library and Theatre
201 East Capitol Street SE
Washington, DC 20003
(202) 544-7077

The Globe Theatre
1107 North Kings Road
Los Angeles, CA 90069
(213) 654-5623

Old Globe Theatre
Balboa Park
San Diego, CA 92112
(619) 231-1941

Oregon Shakespearean Festival
15 South Pioneer
Ashland, OR 97520
(503) 482-2111

Theater Tickets in Britain

Edwards and Edwards
1 Times Square Plaza
New York, NY 10036
(212) 944-0290
(800) 223-6108

Keith Prowse and Co., (USA) Ltd.
234 West 44th Street
New York, NY 10036
(212) 302-7077
(800) 223-4446

Travel

British Airways
1901 Avenue of the Stars
Los Angeles, CA 90067
(800) 247-9297

345 Powell Street
San Francisco, CA 94102
(800) 247-9297

1830 K Street NW
Washington, DC 20006
(800) 247-9297

100 North Biscayne Boulevard
Suite 1315
Miami, FL 33132
(800) 247-9297

67 East Madison Street
Room 2004
Chicago, IL 60603
(800) 247-9297

Sears Crescent Building
City Hall Plaza, 2nd Floor
Boston, MA 02201
(800) 247-9297

400 Renaissance Center
Suite 2210
Detroit, MI 48243
(800) 247-9297

530 Fifth Avenue
New York, NY 10036
(800) 247-9297

1725 John F. Kennedy Boulevard
Philadelphia, PA 19103
(800) 247-9297

1315 4th Avenue
Seattle, WA 98101
(800) 247-9297

British Caledonian Airways
6733 South Sepulveda Boulevard
Los Angeles, CA 90045
(800) 231-0270

777 Cleveland Avenue
Suite 520
Atlanta, GA 30315
(800) 231-0270

1180 Avenue of the Americas
New York, NY 10036
(800) 231-0270

P.O. Box 3156
Fairview Heights
East St. Louis, IL 62208
(800) 231-0270

Interfirst Place
Suite 600
P.O. Box 610647
DFW Airport
Dallas, TX 75261
(800) 392-6650

British Rail
800 South Hope Street
Suite 603
Los Angeles, CA 90017
(213) 626-0088

333 N. Michigan Avenue
Chicago, IL 60601
(312) 263-1910

630 Third Avenue
New York, NY 10017
(212) 599-5400

British Tourist Authority
World Trade Center
Suite 450
350 South Figueroa Street
Los Angeles, CA 90071
(213) 628-3525

John Hancock Center
Suite 3320
875 North Michigan Avenue
Chicago, IL 60611
(312) 787-0490

40 West 57th Street
New York, NY 10019
(212) 581-4700

Cedar Maple Plaza
Suite 210
2305 Cedar Springs Road
Dallas, TX 75201
(214) 720-4040

Cunard
555 Fifth Avenue
New York, NY 10017
(212) 661-7777
(800) 6-CUNARD
The QE2

Ken Leahy
5342 Charmes
Sarasota, FL 33580
(813) 371-8383
British spa tours

Sterling Tours
2707 Congress Street
Suite 1-H
San Diego, CA 92110
(619) 299-3010
(800) 621-0852

Townsend Thoresen
P.O. Box A
Saltillo, PA 17253
(814) 448-3845
Cross-channel ferries

Universal Heritage Tours
64 Main Street
Tuckahoe, NY 10707
(914) 337-5060
(800) 848-6877

Venice Simplon-Orient-Express
One World Trade Center
Suite 1235
New York, NY 10048
(212) 938-6830
(800) 524-2420
Train journeys on the Orient-Express

Williams World Travel, Ltd.
1414 Avenue of the Americas
New York, NY 10019
(212) 752-3525